Book Cover designed by Stan Wooten. Book Artwork by Stan Wooten. Photography and illustrations by Stan Wooten.

Copyright © 2019   Published August 2019

All rights reserved. No portion of this book may be reproduced- mechanically, electronically, or by any other means, including photocopying-without written permission of the author and publisher.

The author is grateful for permission to republish two articles about the former Dallas Apparel Mart by the Dallas Morning News. The author is also grateful to Trammel Crow Holding LLC for permission to republish numerous photos of the former Dallas Apparel Mart.

Request for permission to reproduce material from this book should be sent to:

Permissions

Stan Wooten

P.O. Box 11324

Dallas, TX 75243

jagrox2012@gmail.com

ISBN: 9781086480702

For Joycelen,
To my former Schoolmate
We share a long rich history.
I hope this (my 4th Book brings
Back great memories for you.
enjoy. Stan Wooten

American Made Apparel

The Legacy

The Collapse

A Memoir
By Stan Wooten

Table of Contents

Introduction   7

  I. Genesis   17

      The Ebony Fashion Fair & GQ Magazine Influence   28

  II. The Legacy and The Collapse   45

  III. The Dallas International Apparel Mart   49

      The sights, sounds, and fun on the last day of market

      Photos of the Great Hall

      My involvement with the Apparel Mart

      The apparel manufacturing industry in Dallas

  IV. Working at the Neiman-Marcus Flagship Store   64

      Three part-time jobs to buy my first car

      The aura of Christmas, and Fortnight   80

      Seeing famous movie star John Wayne shopping   81

      Meeting Architect John W. Jones while making a delivery

      Mr. Stanley's Influence   88

  V. The Beecham Sisters; Among Dallas' Finest Seamstresses   94

      Origins sewing blouses of leftover sugar and flour bags

      Industrial sewing classes

Working for Howard Wolf 95

Leadership skills recognized and rewarded

About the great Victor Costa? 99

Aunt Margaret Introduces me to George Scales 100

George Scales Interview 101

VI. Taking Grand Stand Label to the store front window ... 106

   Origins that cultivated confidence in being a good designer

   Art Classes at the Dallas Museum of Art 107

   The Grand Stand Label

   The One Suits (Jump Suits); My first original designs

   Environmental and peer influences on my designs ... 123

VII. Rock Stars Influence on the Fashion World 120

   The Woodstock era rebellion against traditional fashion

   Gentlemen's Quarterly (GQ) magazines influence

   Eccentric fashion Vs. Creative mainstream fashion

VIII. Pro Athletes Influence on the Fashion World 126

   The late Harvey Martin, Too Tall Jones, and me at the Americana

   Michael Jordan's basketball shorts started a worldwide trend

   NBA Sports Announcer Kenny Smith resurrects a twenty-year-old trend

   Kobe Bryant validates Kenny Smith's trend on the cover of GQ magazine

IX. Custom Sportswear for the Cowboy Players   133

    The most challenging anatomy to custom fit.

    Making jackets for the whole team, Super Bowl X and XII

    Making custom two-piece denim and burlap suits

    What you probably didn't know about the late Harvey Martin   135

    What you probably didn't know about Drew Pearson   138

    What you probably didn't know about Too Tall Jones   142

    Things got wild when "Hollywood" Henderson showed up   143

    Hanging out with Tony Dorsett and entourage   150

X. Downs and Walls Sporting Goods Store   151

    Tour guide for Mike, and Everson as we shopped the Apparel Mart

XI. The East Coast Connection   153

    Engineering career move relocates me to Washington DC

    Completes first book

    The international influences of Washington DC on fashion

XII. Passion for Fashion   160

    Family influences passion for fashion (Aunt Rosie)

    Shopping; a favorite past time

    My first Fashion Show with help from friends at The Gazebo   161

XIII. Fashion Detour into the Black Market   164

The many stores, boutiques, and shops on the shopping escapade

Stumbling into counterfeits while shopping in Lower Manhattan

Peak activity for black market fashion merchandise

Black market hustlers profile making $10,000. a day   168
(The names have been changed to protect the innocent)

The risk of severe and exorbitant fines, and legal fees when caught

XIV. The Collapse   181

    Watching the World Cup Soccer games conjures up Patriotism

    The U.S. Trade Deficit with China

    Implications on short term future role of apparel

    Legendary ingenuity is our competitive edge

    Interview with James Baldwin (International Sourcing Agent)   182

    Predictions about the next generation of apparel

    Tips for the next generation of apparel designers, and entrepreneurs

XV. Epilogue   196

    The Desiderata

    In Memoriam Of My Great-Great Grandfather

"American Made Apparel"

"The Legacy - The Collapse"

A Memoir

By Stan Wooten

Introduction

The Dallas International Apparel Mart (Demolished 2006) was the largest, and most spectacular Apparel Mart in the world. It was the supermarket where thousands of retail stores, large, and small, from all over the country, came to buy apparel from manufacturers, and wholesalers. The 1.8 million sq. ft. Apparel Mart (the size of over 36 football fields, in total area) was the economic engine of the Dallas apparel wholesale industry, which was second in the nation, only to New York City.

The unparalleled beauty of the Great Hall was the centerpiece of the facility, and served as a venue for large fashion shows, as well as social, and civic events. Because of its former grandeur, and prominence in the apparel industry, this Apparel Marts demise is symbolic of the failed state of U.S. apparel production vs. what apparel we import (3% vs. 97%). According to the American Apparel and Footwear Association (AAFA), we Americans now spend close to $400 Billion a year for clothing, and footwear in this country. 97% of the apparel we buy is imported and factors heavily against the United States $225 Billion trade deficit with China.

This book tells why we should be very concerned about the economic consequences of such circumstances and pursue alternatives to our current course.

"American Made Apparel" a memoir, focuses on the legacy of high fashion apparel manufacturing in Dallas,TX, as author Stan Wooten, tells the story of being born into a family of seamstresses who made clothing for the most elite retail stores in America, such as Neiman-Marcus, Sak's, Bloomingdale's, and Macy's. As a sixteen-year-old, the author was the Downtown delivery boy for the Neiman Marcus flagship store, in downtown Dallas. Neiman-Marcus has long been considered the best specialty store in the world. This memoir shares stories about movie superstars, like King of the Cowboys, John Wayne, when they came shopping where the author worked.

"American Made Apparel" chronicles the story of the Authors three aunts who were highly skilled seamstresses. One of the aunts owned and operated a sewing school, and the other two owned, and operated contract sewing shops, with contracts from top designers like Victor Costa, whose dresses were sold in the very best retail stores in the country. The authors aunt also had an exclusive contract with Neiman Marcus to sew dresses made of imported European & Asian fabrics.

At the age of twenty-two, he joined his aunts in the apparel manufacturing business, and started his own line of Men's Sportswear (Grand Stand), outfitting the Super Bowl Champion, Dallas Cowboys Team, for three years, and two Super Bowls. The Grand Stand label designs were shown in the showrooms of the Apparel Mart during its peak activity. The book shows photos of clothing made for Cowboy Super Bowl teams, in 1976 thru 1978.

In 1982 Stan Wooten was General Managing Partner of Downs and Walls Sporting Goods, a partnership with Dallas Cowboys Micheal Downs, and Super Bowl Champion, All-Pro Everson Walls. During this period of time he was a buyer at the Apparel Mart, and the first stages of decline had begun to show in the business activity at the Apparel Mart.

The book presents several stunningly beautiful pictures of The Dallas International Apparel Mart. So impressive was this building that the 1977 science fiction thriller movie "Logans Run" filmed a significant part of their movie in the Great Hall (the focus of the photos).

The book examines in detail, the decline of American Made Apparel, and how that decline has fueled the sales of counterfeit, and Black-Market fashion products worldwide. Because manufacturers throughout Asia do not respect US copyright laws, the stage was set for hard working Americans who might otherwise be unemployed, to make more than $10,000. a day in the Black Market.

"American Made Apparel - The Legacy-The Collapse" shares the authors rapport with the late Mr. Stanley Marcus (April 20, 1905 – January 24, 2002), long after he stopped working for the store. A well-kept secret that Mr. Stanley shared with the author in private, is presented in detail.

The book features a special dedication to Stanley Marcus, celebrating his huge influence on the social fabric of the city that he loved, the authors' hometown, Dallas, TX. The most outstanding thing about Stanley Marcus for the author was, "in addition to being the absolute most gifted merchant in history, he was sensitive to the fact that the overall social fabric of the city would be enhanced by elevating socio-economic opportunities for African Americans, and other minorities." "He made it his business to address this dysfunction, and did not allow his wealth, and privileged Harvard education to make him insensitive to the big picture;

the overall quality of life in Dallas, and our nation as a whole" said the author.

"The late Stanley Marcus was an unsung hero in the Civil Rights movement of the 60's" said the author. "Not only did Mr. Stanley hire many African Americans at Neiman-Marcus, but in 1967 he also encouraged all of the 5000 suppliers and vendors selling to his stores, to do the same". (Ref. "Minding The Store", pg. 370, The Memoir by Stanley Marcus).

This book presents facts that most people didn't know about Dallas legend, the late Harvey Martin, who died of pancreatic cancer December 24, 2001. Harvey was not only a Super Bowl MVP for the Cowboys; he was a good friend of the author since Zumwalt Junior High School. Harvey was the primary reason the author got an opportunity to produce clothing for the Cowboys team, and subsequently make custom garments for Harvey and his many teammates. Harvey still holds the NFL record for quarterback sacks in a single season, although the NFL did not count quarterback sacks until 1982, the Cowboys credited Harvey with 23 sacks in 1977-78, the year he was Super Bowl MVP. To this day no NFL defensive player besides Harvey has ever had more than 22.5 sacks in one season.

The book reveals behind the scenes details to the Dallas Cowboys locker room, and the real-life party details not seen since "North Dallas Forty" a novel written by former Cowboy receiver Pete Gent which was made into a 1979 motion picture.

The book reveals dresses that the authors Aunt Margaret and her sewing crew made for Neiman-Marcus, that were sold in the stores for $200., and at J.C. Penney's for $50. The only difference was the label. (This was an anomaly, not the rule. Neiman-Marcus quality and customer service has always been superior).

"American Made Apparel" exposes behind the scenes stories of several real-life Black-Market hustlers making $10,000. a day, selling designer replica/black market purses, jewelry, watches, and sunglasses.   The Author explains the reason so many of the rich and famous blend replicas into their wardrobes.

While the Author does not condone or promote the illicit sales of counterfeits, and in fact discourages such activity, he does acknowledge the proliferation of such products to mainstream America over the last three decades. There are extenuating, and complex circumstances currently forcing a change in the apparel manufacturing industry. Collaborating with a captain of the international industrial complex, the author explains in detail the evolution of the apparel manufacturing business, how the Mafia's $60million a year extortion, changed the Garment District in New York in the 70s, and what forces are today changing the industry once again.

This book will elevate constructive dialog towards a viable solution of black-market goods vs. limited domestic manufacturing opportunities in the high fashion apparel industry. More importantly the book celebrates the rich legacy that Dallas has in the High Fashion Apparel Industry.

Because we discuss money in this book, I thought it would help to have some context. The following five – 3-D illustrations help clarify a few important facts.

$10,000 - Enough for a great vacation or to buy a used car.

$1,000,000. ONE MILLION DOLLARS.
You could stuff this into a duffle bag.

$100,000,000 ONE HUNDRED MILLION DOLLARS
Starting to get interesting now?
The couch is made from $46.7 million of crispy $100 bills.

$1,000,000,000 $1Billion
You are looking at 10 tons of $100. bills on those pallets. Now we are talking mega bucks.

There are no Trillionaires!   Not even one.

I don't think anyone on the planet has ever actually seen this much money at one time.

Genesis

My mother and father were both born in rural small towns of east Texas. Avinger, Texas population 489 is where my mother Johnnie Mae Goss Wooten was born. With her family, she moved to Dallas as a toddler.

My father Lee Wooten Jr. was born in Lovelady, Texas population 640, and for sure both places were what we all called "the country." My Dad moved to Dallas as a teenager along with his first cousin Bedford Butler, and both came to join my Dads older sister Rosie, who had recently moved to Dallas. For decades prior to my birth in 1952, cotton crops were king in Texas, and cotton fields were the life blood of most small rural towns even through the early 1950s.

There is a good reason that the world-famous football stadium at the State Fair of Texas is called the Cotton Bowl. Cotton was king in Texas, even more so than peaches are to Georgia, or oranges are to Florida. There were trucks that picked up workers to take to the fields every morning and bring them back in the evenings. Poor black families in those days used virtually every able body in their family to gain bigger loads and make more money. Men, women, boys, and girls; age didn't matter; all that mattered is that you pick, pull, or chop cotton, so I'm told by eyewitnesses. Wages, for lack of a better term were low, but so was the cost of living. If a family pulled together and worked hard, they could buy a car, or truck, and many of them did just that. Bigger families were more successful at this, because they depended on each other more.

This was the reality for the vast majority of Black people in small rural towns throughout Texas, and much of the south. Even in a big city like Dallas, I am told that there were trucks which came to pick up workers for suburban cotton fields in locations right outside of the of Dallas city limits. Amazing to think that Political, Leaders like the late Tom Bradley former Mayor of LA, the late Percy Sutton (the Beloved Prince of Harlem) and Willie Brown (Former mayor of San Francisco) all hailed from this culture.

Being born in 1952 at Parkland Hospital, the same hospital that President Kennedy was rushed to after he was assassinated in Dallas, I was the first one in my family to never step one foot into a cotton field.

My Mom and Dad were fully intent on gaining a higher quality of life in the bigger cities, than what smaller towns like the ones they left behind could offer.

With hard work and many blessings, Mom and Dad made good on their mission. Dallas offered an abundance of opportunities to make a living, and they both worked low wage jobs to support our family of four. My Dad worked two jobs for most of his life.

Both my older sister Vivian, and I attended a private school before going to Dallas Public schools three years later. Immaculate Heart of Mary is the name of my first school. It is a Catholic school. We wore uniforms every day, and the school was very discipline focused.

The Nunn's who taught us at the school were called sisters, and they gave us very detailed rules, of do's and don'ts, and violations meant physical punishment. Whacks on the knuckles with a ruler, or pulling and twisting your ear loaf, seemed to be the Sisters favorite punishment for rule breakers. That's what I remember most about that school.

My next school was N.W. Harllee elementary. That is where my personality began to develop. We had very encouraging teachers, who were enthusiastic about their student's potential. They pushed, pulled, and challenged students to attain a solid education while having fun in the process.

We would take field trips to the Museum of Natural History, Dallas Museum of Art, The Symphony Orchestra, and even one extraordinary trip to Carlsbad Caverns in New Mexico when I was in fifth grade.

My mom was very involved with the school's PTA and had rapport with all of the teachers for my sister Vivian, and myself. I can clearly remember how much fun it was to see my Mom and other mothers participating in a play produced to entertain the students and faculty, one night at the school auditorium. The I Love Lucy style play, was entertaining and so funny, featuring a cast of 10 mothers of students at the school. Priceless!! I don't know who came up with the idea, but it was definitely a winner.

The music teacher, Mr. Henry was the consummate gentleman, a most enthusiastic, inspiring, and energetic man, who thought he could turn on some kind of magical button in me so that I would be converted to a good singer. After months of futility at this hopeless endeavor, Mr. Henry seemed to be convinced that it was pointless.

He then recruited me for the Cub Scout group that he led. This was fun; a small group of about 10 boys, 7 to 10 years-old dressed in our blue and gold Cub Scout uniforms, with caps and yellow handkerchiefs around the neck, would march to the nearby park after school, and cook hotdogs over a camp fire, while we listened to lessons on becoming a good scout. How cool.

The teachers at N.W. Harllee seemed to be on a mission to unlock some kind of hidden talent in students, and my art teacher took some pretty extreme measures in this pursuit. We didn't just get challenged with drawing in pencil, ink, and crayons coloring, but painting with watercolors, acrylic, and oil, paper mache, plaster of Paris, and sculpting, as well as etching. This was all part of the curriculum, and really fascinated me.

We discovered my passion, and talent for art. In a relatively short time, my pencil portraits of President John F. Kennedy garnered much praise from my art teacher and classmates and were showcased in the school's trophy case. Shortly afterwards my plaster of Paris sculpture which was painted in acrylic, along with a large ink and crayon etching were also showcased. I still have them in my collection to this day.

My family was traditional southern Baptist; and for a child that meant from the time you were old enough to string five or six words together you were put in front of the church congregation to say a speech at special occasions, Christmas, Easter, Pastors anniversary, etc. We all called it a program. Lil Stanley is going to be on a program.

I was never thrilled about standing in front of a whole congregation of mostly adults to give a speech, but I watched my other family members do it with ease and grace. As a matter of fact my sister and cousins were very good at public speaking even in their youth. My cousin John Etta became an excellent public speaker, and the quintessential church lady, even better than many preachers at public speaking.

Somehow, I was included in the oratorical contest held at our school, either voluntarily or selected by my teacher, I can't remember which. My sister was also selected for the same contest in a higher-grade level. My speech was selected by my English teacher. She chose a poem by Langston Hughes entitled "I too Sing America". I was the darkest complexioned member of my immediate family, but in my extended family, I was only outdone in this category by my bold and beautiful first cousin Eunice.

My dark complexion didn't bother me at all. It never really crossed my mind, especially because I was only eight years old. However, in retrospect when I read the poem, I can't help but feel that either the speech was chosen, or I was chosen due in some part to my very dark complexion. You be the judge. The short poem follows:

I, too, sing America.
I am the darker brother.
They send me to eat in the kitchen
when company comes,
but I laugh,
and eat well,
and grow strong.
Tomorrow,
I'll be at the table
when company comes.
Nobody'll dare
Say to me,
"Eat in the kitchen,"
Then they'll see how beautiful I am
and be ashamed--
I, too, sing America.

By Langston Hughes

My sister Vivian won a second-place trophy in her grade level, and I won a first-place trophy in my grade level in this contest, and every other oratorical contest that I competed in during my school days.

As an 8, year old, this was all just big fun for me, and I loved the results, however things were about to change when I discovered the love of my life. No, it wasn't a girl. It was basketball.

My dad bought a basketball and goal and put the goal on a nice backboard, and goal post, in our backyard, which was more than big enough to handle a half court. A neighbor named James Johnson – nicknamed Cuda - who was three years older than me and lived in a house on the next street over, would stop by almost daily to give me some pointers on how to shoot the ball properly.

Our backyards were separated by the alley. In a very short time I caught on, and basketball became my favorite past-time. Our backyard became the neighborhood park, and I frequently played with the schools sixth grade team, although I was only in the third grade. This went on for years afterward, and I would play basketball after school in that backyard until dark.

When my friends would go home at dusk dark, I would typically shoot basketball all alone under moonlight. I had a bad case of the basketball jones. By the time I was in 6th grade, I was averaging 28 points per game, and the leading scorer of all the players in my grade level, for all the teams we played.

My early success cemented my love affair with basketball. This is an excellent example of what happens when people attain goals and rewards for achieving something they really enjoy anyway. It deepens our passion for that thing, whatever it is. Thank God for James "Cuda" Johnson. Had he not come along when he did, right after my Dad put our basketball goal up, I might have developed some really bad shooting habits right from the start, that would have been hard to break.

There were no other basketball players in our family at the time. I was the first. Cuda was the only person I knew who could teach an eight-year-old like me, the right way to shoot, and play basketball. Without his help I doubt if I would have developed a good shot so fast. Although I was an early bloomer who peaked soon, and wasn't good enough to play professionally, a few of my teammates did play in the NBA - Kenneth "Grasshopper" Smith of the San Antonio Spurs, and Ira Terrell of the Portland Trailblazers - and I celebrate with no envy, their well-deserved success.

Basketball was, and still is the love of my life. I still play 3 to 4 days a week. Through playing basketball, I have met many good friends for a lifetime, starting with Mr. Horton, my first basketball coach.

In the early 60s there was a lot going on in the background that I knew about but was not sure what to make of it. Little did I know that much of what happened culturally in the 60s, music, politics, art & high fashion apparel, and automobiles production, would have enormous impact on not only my life, but the whole country for decades, if not centuries to come? Simply put the 60s were a revolutionary time, and a time of renaissance all rolled up into one big package. We had the good, the bad, the brilliant, and the ugly.

There are volumes of history books on the 60s, and the facts are well documented, so I won't bore you with well-known details, yet there are several vital points worth noting. The 60s music still has major relevance today. The Motown groups like the Temptations, Stevie Wonder, Marvin Gaye, Michael Jackson, and the Jackson five, are all unsurpassed in their achievements, even though they came on the scene over fifty years ago.

The same can be said for The Beatles, The Rolling Stones, and Jimi Hendrix. The 1969 Woodstock music festival became one of the biggest (a half million people) and most successful concerts in history. The Rock & Roll revolution was firmly established yet clearly drew from a wide range of indigenous music forms such as traditional blues, rhythm and blues, jazz, gospel, folk music, country, and even classical (the Moody Blues).

The 60s Rock music influenced the cultures art, fashion, and politics, and of course in return it was influenced by the current events of the times. Events such as the Viet Nam war, the civil rights struggle for racial equality, and the assassinations of JFK, MLK, and RFK were creatively made into protest songs about freedom.

There has not been a time in our nation's history, neither before, nor since the 60s where there was such a homogenization of music styles that formed under the big umbrella of Rock and Roll. The R&B music which was clearly established by the likes of Motown, Stax, and Chess Records, also secured its place in history as pioneers of popular music worldwide.

OK, I think you get my point. To grow up witnessing so much history in the making was a privilege that I cherish.

My Mom was a jazz, and blues lover, and she had a collection of albums by Miles Davis, Dave Brubeck (Take 5), Wes Montgomery, Cannonball Adderly, and Lou Rawls. This was my soundtrack at 8 to 14 years old. My mom was pretty classy huh? My Dad liked music too, but no blues, just happy music, as he put it. However, my Dad didn't buy music, because "he preferred spending his surplus funds on beer", is how Mom put it.

Even as a nine-year-old I knew there were a lot of hot button issues happening from seeing the tension in my parent's expression when they watched the TV news reports. They would talk to me about some of the issues briefly, but would tell me to go do my homework, or something, brushing me off. Walter Cronkite was the go-to guy for news. He was the most trustworthy reporter on TV during those times.

So trustworthy was Walter Cronkite, that he earned the nickname of Uncle Walter, by many households across the nation. I totally understand the nickname, because he and my uncle Cleveland Baker who was a very well-respected man, had very similar features, and demeanor, even though they are of different races.

TV broadcast were not our only source for news. Fortunately, my parents kept a subscription to a collection of magazines, such as Life, Time, Ebony, Jet, and especially for me MAD magazine, and Sports Illustrated once it became clear that I had a basketball jones. We also had subscriptions to the daily local newspaper (The Dallas Times Herald), and the weekly black newspaper (The Post Tribune).

The freedoms that we all take for granted nowadays were certainly not a given in the early 60s. Most people who were born after the early 60s cannot imagine the indignity of being denied service at any little fast food restaurant or denied the use of a public restroom because of the color of your skin.

This was an everyday occurrence in the life of black people, who had no legal recourse against being denied entrance at Neiman-Marcus, or any other retail establishment. Seeking a job at many businesses was totally out of the question, because they had an open clearly stated policy of not hiring African Americans, and their discrimination was sanctioned by law. I take no pleasure in pointing out these simple facts, but it is fundamental to understanding why the civil rights movements of the 60s was one of the most monumental cultural movements in our nation's history. Unfortunately, far too many citizens of the U.S.A. fail to understand the core principles of that movement.

As I grew older, I began to pay more attention to the news, especially when I noticed that there were a lot of people who looked like me getting beat up by policemen. I noticed that big police dogs like "Tip" the German Shepard police dog we had in the back yard, were being used to attack unarmed people who were marching in peaceful protest.

When that became clear to me, I was 9 or 10 years old. From that point on I began to pay close attention to the TV news, magazines, and newspapers, trying to understand what the hell was going on. It was not long before I knew who Martin Luther King Jr. was.

At first notion from my 9-year-old eyes he was just the little black man who was always getting beat up and getting the big police dogs sicked on him. It did not take much more reading and listening to find out why he was so hated by racist.

In the 60s Ebony/Jet magazines were the go-to source for news, sports, and fashion, featuring the biggest African American movie stars, super star athletes, super star musicians, and artist, as well as politicians and scholars. Their lifestyles focus, and the Ebony Fashion Fair showcased the latest designs in the world of High Fashion especially for women.

The Ebony Fashion Fair was the biggest traveling fashion show in the world, regularly showing 200 or more garments in each show. There was always a theatrical presentation to Ebony's fashion shows. They were the first to use music for runway models. The fashion shows featured garments by top European designers such as Karl Lagerfeld, Yves St. Laurent, Emanuel Ungaro, Oscar De Larenta, Pierre Cardin, Christian Lacroix, and American Bill Blass, as well as two of the top African American designers Stephen Burrows, and Patrick Kelly, and other lesser known designers.

When I saw the artistry of high fashion apparel, even as a 10-year-old, I believe my fascination with art was transferred to apparel. I clearly remember that clothing was always important in my family.

Just for kicks my teenage cousin, Willie Dee Ellison used to walk three blocks from their house to ours each Sunday morning, and help me get dressed for church. Willie Dee usually brought something new like a necktie or cuff links for me to wear. He probably knew that he was going to be gone soon, but I didn't. Within weeks Willie Dee left home for boot camp in the Army. He was one of over a dozen soldiers (Marines, Sailors, and only one Airman) in my family. Those happy days, where he was so kind to me was all I have left to remember of him.

He was an overweight young man, and oddly drowned to death in an accident while on leave back in Dallas. There is no doubt that my parents and relatives influenced me to some extent, yet my passion for fashion became apparent to me at around ten years old when I began to tell my mom I wanted to pick my own clothes. The colors were very important to me.

By the time I was eleven, I was very aware of all the relatives who were well dressed, Mom and Dad's friends, and our neighbors. I knew the older boys in the neighborhood who were well dressed. I knew who was cool, who had Flava, and Swag. At 11 years old, I wanted to have more money, more money to buy more clothes. That little $1.50 a week allowance that my parents gave me wasn't cutting it.

I would have gotten more had I made more A's on my report cards, but that just wasn't happening. I got permission from my parents to get a paper route with the local African American weekly newspaper, The Post Tribune. That worked out fine for a while.

About that time, I started noticing older guys wearing the coolest stainless steel, ID bracelets with their initials engraved on them, and tinted lens eyeglasses. Next it was the teal colored (turquoise) cotton pullover hoodie, no other color would do. I know I was driving my Mom crazy, but I was so sincere about all of this.

My sister Vivian who was five years older than me, got her first part time job at sixteen, and she wanted to buy her little brother something with her first check. I was so lucky back then. Wow, how sweet. Lucky me at eleven years old. I told her exactly what I wanted down to a tee. I completely described the style, material, brand, color, size, and exactly where to buy it. I think I broke her from ever again volunteering to buy whatever little brother wanted. From that point on, she never asked me what I wanted; she just bought her choice, which was usually not a fashion item like shirts, or pants, but accessories, and underwear.

I really wanted those tinted lens eyeglasses; they came in three colors, green, blue, and rose tint. I scouted them out at Texas State Optical. They were not cheap, and my little weekly paper route money wasn't cutting it.

For anyone who doubts the overwhelming influence of the muscle cars of the sixties, I challenge you to name just one single car made in another decade that remains a top seller 50 years later, and had its own hit R&B/Pop record like the Ford Mustang, and Mustang Sally by the legendary "Wicked Wilson Pickett".

Wilson Pickett was a bona-fide Soul Man, who didn't have the body of work of a James Brown, or Aretha Franklin. However, like other soul men such as Otis Redding, Sam & Dave, Sam Cook, and Lil Johnnie Taylor, just to name a few, they made tremendous contributions to the soul music frontier of the 60s.

They were soul music pioneers, and their influence is still felt and heard fifty years later through the music of top R&B artist like Charlie Wilson.

The 60's as you know, was characterized as the most turbulent and violent decade in modern history. However, it was the most productive decade in many ways, and it produced our 44th president (President Obama) who was born in 1961. The assassination of President John F. Kennedy in 1963, was a sad, and shocking event for everyone I knew. It was especially crushing for me, because I believed the hopes, and dreams of racial equality would be suppressed with his death. I cried and grieved as though I had lost a family member, and so did almost everyone I knew.

The African American community loved and revered JFK more than any previous President, and he was a hero. In virtually every home that I visited through the 70's, relatives, friends, and even strangers I would always see photos, or statues of JFK, flanked by Martin Luther King and Robert Kennedy.

He was by far my all-time favorite person to draw portraits of. It might have been because it was easy for me to reinterpret his distinct facial qualities, yet I have not drawn portraits of anyone, the way that I did of President John F. Kennedy since those days in the early 60's. My former classmates still talk about those portraits, to this day.

It was President John F. Kennedy who said, "Those who make peaceful revolution impossible, make violent revolution inevitable."

In a nutshell, this was the cause, and effect of the many race riots that swept across America. The oppression was relentless. I know this fact from experience. Imagine a 5-year-old little boy being hit with an umbrella by an old white-haired senior citizen White woman, who said "get to the back of the bus you little nigger". It's not hard for me to imagine, because I was that 5-year-old boy. In reference to the aforementioned quote by President Kennedy, the race riots that raged in big cities, created a dilemma for America of no justice, no peace. "No justice, no peace" was not just a chant, or slogan, it was a promise that was easy to believe coming from those who were determined to continue literally fighting against racial oppression.

Their position contrasted Dr. King and his peaceful freedom riders. Either one of these rather large factions of civil rights defenders, the ones the media called militants, or the freedom riders who marched with Dr. King, would not have presented much of a dilemma as a solo act. However, the constant threat of riots destroying communities in major cities across the nation set up a dilemma.

Fiery activist like The Black Panthers, Malcolm X, Stokley Carmicheal, and H. Rap Brown made their voices heard thru the media. All of these characters were brought into our living room everyday by none other than "the most trusted man in America", Uncle Walter. There were many heros and sheros in the civil rights movement besides Dr. King.

We saw them frequently on Walter Cronkites news reports. For a fact the civil rights struggle started long before the 60's, and before MLK came along, however his leadership was indispensable, and certainly enhanced the movement.

In the early 60s I would spend a portion of my summer vacation with my Aunt Rosie and her family who lived in Bon-Ton, which was the toughest Projects in Dallas (bar-none). We were a tight knit family and spent almost every Sunday evening together. My father and his sister (Aunt Rosie) were inseparable. My Aunt Rosie had four children, yet only three lived with her, because her oldest (Eural) had married and moved away. They were all older than me, with the youngest boy (Edward) being a High

School student. During my summer stay the plan was that I was to follow Edward around, and hang out with him a little, and not get into any trouble, and my oldest cousin Lizzie Mae would see to it that I got good meals, and snacks.

My cousin Edward was something like a celebrity at Lincoln High School, where he was a leader of the ROTC Drill Team marching performance group known as the Black Knights. They would perform at school football games and in downtown parades on Main Street, at the start of the State Fair. Seeing that group perform all their moves, and choreographed precision drills, was more like a college fraternity step show, than a drill team. It was an awesome sight to see for everyone, especially a third grader like me.

My cousin Edward was the leader and we were all very proud of him. Well everything went fine for a while, but Edward and his pals got this bright idea to put me into fights against the other little boys in the neighborhood who were my age. They would bet spare change on the fights and cheer me on.

The fights were never really bloody, but still real fights just for entertainment of my cousin and his pals. I thought it was cool, because I thought my cousin was so cool. This went on for three or four days a week, and I won every fight. One day we crossed the path of a little boy who was really scared and tried to get away from the fight. I remember this like yesterday. I pushed the little boy and dared him to fight. As he turned to retreat, and tried to escape the fight, the little boy's sister grabbed him, and shouted "you better fight". "You know what Mama told you, if you don't fight back, you're gonna get a whippin" the little boy began to cry because he was between a rock and a hard place.

His sister shook him by the shoulders and shouted, "you fight!!!" The little boy clutched his fist, closed his eyes, and lunged at me whirling a hard, swift, windmill of desperate blows to my face and head. Next thing I know, I was on the ground for the first time in all my fights. No Mas-No Mas! I knew nothing about a comeback, or any type of fight strategy. My trainers never mentioned that. I guess they just figured I was a natural. That pretty much wrapped up my career as a 9-year-old prize fighter.

I learned that fighting people, who are desperately scared to death of you, can be hazardous to your health. My cousin Ed was a little wild, but he wasn't crazy. Ed joined the Navy right after he graduated from High School. After a successful tour of duty in the Navy, he returned home to Dallas, began a long career at American Airlines, got married and started a family. He bought a brand-new Ford Mustang shortly after he returned home and would periodically come and take me to the Dallas Cowboys football games with him and his pals.

For sure being ready willing, and able to defend yourself was part of the survival kit for boys growing up in places like Bon-Ton, or most urban communities. There would be other times later in my life when older boys who had influence over the youngsters, would pit us against each other to fight for their entertainment.

It was only months after the JFK assassination that my parents decided to move to South Oak Cliff (S.O.C.) a very big newly integrated neighborhood. This was all unprecedented by-products of the new Fair Housing Act, which made it a violation of the law to refuse to sell or rent a house to someone because of race.

South Central Dallas (South Oak Cliff) was 75,000 people and 90% White in 1962, and by 1972 it was 215,000 people and 90% African American. There were a lot more apartments. That's kind of how integration worked in Dallas, TX during those days. Blacks move in, and the Whites move out. It was called White flight. I transferred to Harry Stone elementary school in its first year of integration (1964). Our school had three White students and no White teachers at all.

My elementary school was only four blocks from our house, so I walked to school each day. The junior high school (Sarah Zumwalt) which sat right in front of our elementary school was still all White and not integrated yet. Predictably there were older White bullies at the junior high school who attacked some of the younger Black students as they walked along the sidewalk, in route to the elementary school. It is still a mystery to me why there was no adult supervision out on the sidewalks to avoid these very predictable conflicts. However, it didn't last long. Three days maximum, and here is why; The makeup of the new SOC was people mostly from the east, west, and south, Dallas Projects. My new neighborhood had more than our share of that type, so Wolf, and T-Monk found out what was going on at that school.

Talking bout, the ghetto. That incident really brought the ghetto out of them. They brutally cleared the sidewalks for two days, and from that point on, no more junior high school bullies blocking the sidewalks for us elementary students.

Fortunately, I was never attacked physically like some of the smaller kids, although I was verbally harassed with the typical hateful racial slurs.

That junior high school (Sarah Zumwalt) which was 100% White, would be integrated the next year, and again I would be in the first class of black students to attend the school, which would turn out to be 97% Black as soon as it was integrated.

The new house was slightly used, but really nice, with a very big back yard. I was losing my basketball court from the old neighborhood, and the hill in our new backyard kind of disqualified it for a replacement.

However, there was a neighborhood park two blocks away, with a descent basketball court. South Oak Cliff was really large, with a lot of undeveloped land. The most progressive young Black families who were aggressively pursuing a higher quality of life for their family, were the ones you would typically find in South Oak Cliff.

People came from all over town; South Dallas (which is very different from South Oak Cliff. The natives all know this) East Dallas, West Dallas, and Oak Cliff, where we moved from. The confluence of so many different neighborhoods was a recipe for conflict. For my first four years in our new neighborhood when I was 12 to 16 years old, I had fights two or three times a week.

I fought more than anybody I knew, and I wasn't a bully. Maybe it was the wild age group that I was in. Sometimes I would fight the same guy two days in a row. There were some really crazy people in the neighborhood, who are virtually all dead or in prison now. In a strange contrast to this story, my graduating class of 1971, has the highest number of professionals of any S.O.C. graduating class.

Our class of 1971 includes several Doctors, Dentist, Engineers, Accountants, Pastors, Business Managers, and no Lawyers thank God, but a lot of respectable citizens. Love you S.O.C. '71.

I never saw so much fighting in my life. 1967-68 I saw students, fighting students (I was in more than my fair share of those), students fighting teachers, and when I got to High School the next year, I even saw students fighting Principals.

The same boy who fought me two days in a row - which wasn't unusual, except that he was fighting the first day only to study my fighting technique – somehow got into a fight with the science teacher, who was a very laid back, and peaceful gentleman. After one or two, quick licks were passed, I can't remember who hit who first, because it happened so fast, but in a matter of seconds, the 14-year-old had the teacher in a head lock. They tussled about for a bit, but it was clear that the student had control of the teacher, with a firm head lock under his right arm. The teacher struggled somewhat passively trying to move towards the door, which opened to the hallway, and said to the student who had him in a headlock, "come on let's go to the Principals office right now" (like he was in control). That's when the whole classroom burst out in laughter. That was the wildest thing I ever saw in a classroom, and it was funny because it wasn't really violent.

After a fight with that same 14-year-old boy, he told me, "I could have beat you yesterday, but I just wanted to see how you fight. I can show you what I'm talking about right now. Just you and me, let's go around to the side of the school, but don't try to pull a gun, because I got mine with me". We went, and he showed me what he was talking about. I got beat, convincingly.

He probably went over my tendencies in his head for hours the night before finding me first thing the next morning, instead of studying his school homework. His priorities probably have a lot do with him being in prison today. The back to back fights usually occurs when someone thought they could have won if they had not slipped or something. To have a fight just to study an opponent's tendencies was really crazy to me, but that's just how crazy things were.

To complicate matters even more, my basketball coach who had a very high profile in town, also a big 6'-7" former college basketball star, and highly respected, would tell us at 13-14years old, "if you know you got to fight, you through the first punch, and make him feel you, cause if you don't, it might be your last punch".

Not only that, he said, "if you got to fight, don't be like the idiots who face off each other, and duel to the death; be like the Indians, and surprise attack; you pick the time, the place, and the circumstances". Wow!!

Thanks Coach Wiley. I never forgot those lessons, and they got me in so much trouble it would make your head swim.

It was someone in the family, one of my many macho cousins, I'm not sure which one, who told me at 12 years old that "if someone throws a rock at you, you throw a brick at them. They'll think twice before they throw a rock at you again". Wow!! How well I remember this lesson. This sounds just like something my cousin Wilmer (one of the first Marines to fight in Viet Nam), would say.

This credo brought so much trouble into my life. With life lessons like these, it should come as no surprise that I was not a fan of Martin Luther Kings' passive resistance and turn the other cheek antics in the civil rights struggle. Dr. Martin Luther King Jr. is recognized worldwide as the undisputed greatest champion of civil rights in America. I understand, and respect what he stood for much better as an adult.

To coach Wiley's credit, I think I can safely say that he was not the best role model in the world, but he taught me a great deal about a strong work ethic, overcoming adversity in life, and determination. I can still remember the quote posted on his desk; "small minds discuss people, average minds discuss events, great minds discuss ideas."

Coach Wiley loaned me money to rush the production thru of my big order for the Dallas Cowboys Super Bowl jackets in 1976. He came to visit my cutting contractor's production shop and gave me my last coaching session with the loan. It went something like this. "Boy, you know where to put this money to make this deal work, don't you?" I replied, yes sir.

"Boy, these people say you a hustler. You got what it takes boy. You get out there and make this deal work!" I owe him a great deal of gratitude. I will never forget him.

My passion for fashion was raging during this period of time, and so were the outside influences from my peers. I met Lil Tim Jackson in my junior high school, who later became Too Tall Jones personal Tailor. Lil Tim is also my pick as the all-time best dressed boy in Dallas public schools. I also met Harvey Martin who became a good friend, and a Super Bowl MVP for the Dallas Cowboys, and my good friend Rickey Roach who became a successful Podiatrist. By the way I never had any fights with these guys. I was an average student at school, doing what I needed to do, to get B's, even though I could have really applied myself, and earned A's. Things were going along fine on the basketball court, and I was getting a lot of attention from girls, so I thought the A's could wait a while.

At 14-years-old I was leading the inner-city schools that we played against in scoring for my grade level. Things were going so good for me that Coach Wiley told my mother at a PTA event that I was good enough to play in the NBA one day **if I stayed on course**. This was big because Coach Wiley had coached high school players who were All-State, and really had pro potential.

There was something really churning away at me inside, seeing Lil Tim, and Bimbo - who was another well-dressed guy at school - showing up wearing those alligator shoes. Both Tim and Bimbo were two grades higher than me. Even though I had something similar to everything else Lil Tim and Bimbo wore, I just had to have some alligator shoes. They were not cheap, so I knew that meant I was going to have to find a way, and I did. At only 14 years old I found several restaurants who would let me work as a bus boy on the weekends during the school year. It wasn't long before I got those alligator shoes, and even more clothes.

By the way it became clear to me about 15 years ago that I have had a whole lot of jobs since starting to work public jobs at 14 years old. My successful oratorical contest skills were paying off, and the template was developed for me to get jobs when I pursued them aggressively.

Over the next two years from 14 years to 16 years old, I bought three pairs of alligator shoes, suits, blazers, Sansabelt slacks, Banana Skins slacks, Italian knit shirts, leather jackets, and suede front sweaters, from some of the best stores downtown. By the way my shopping habits were not totally unusual back then.

There were 14-16-year old's all over town spending some serious cash on clothes very much like what I bought. However, they were not buying from Neiman-Marcus, and they were buying on a smaller scale.

I had been bugging my parents about a car since I was 14 years old, and they would just kind of just brush it off. I kept telling them about a classmate of mine who had his own car at 13 years old.

They were not impressed, and they told me I would have to wait. My sister, who is five years older, got her first car right after graduating high school. She liked me, and I knew it, so I talked her into letting me drive her 1962 Chevy Impala every now and then. At 16 I had stepped my game up on the court, and the streets, going to night clubs and parties every weekend. I had a steady girlfriend who was a real cutie, and we were in love.

My academic work was still average, and I was doing what was necessary to get by. I wasn't fighting as much thank God. My sophomore year at SOC was when I got the bright idea to try and get a summer job at Neiman-Marcus, and lucky me, I got it. Needless to say, my wardrobe got a big boast, with my 25% employee discount. I planned my purchases for the biggest sales' promotional events, and I would then use my 25% employee discount.

My girlfriend and I, both had a passion for fashion that was in high gear during that period. Working weekends, and Thursday nights, at Neiman-Marcus during the school year, and two other part-time jobs cleaning an office building, and a Doubleday Book Store at night during the week, I built up a descent savings for a car down payment.

My parents knew that I was determined, because I was showing responsibility by earning my own money, so they agreed to sign for the 1968 Pontiac Firebird I picked. I waited for my income tax return to come in, so that I could combine it with my savings and make a substantial down payment. It worked out pretty well, because my monthly payments were only $68.11 a month. Wow!! You got to love the value of a dollar in 1969. With only 1100 miles on it, my car cost $3,200.

There was one more big fight at school that led to me being expelled. Unfortunately for me it was right before our varsity basketball team played for the city championship in 1969. I would have been one of only two sophomores on our varsity team rooster. The fight started over my watch that had a spider web design on the face, yet it looked like a Cartier tank watch, or Longines, which was a pretty popular watch at the time. Almost everybody who saw my watch raved about how beautiful and special it was. I bought it at Neiman-Marcus. The two guys who stole it were pretending to be playing with me, tussling as one of them (who I knew well, and thought he was my friend) unbuckled it, and slipped it of my arm.

I didn't know until hours later that my watch was gone.

I realized that it was two of them, and just one of me. They were both seniors, and I was just a sophomore. All I could think about was the rock, and the brick lesson. This was one of the times my better judgment served me well, because I didn't let my anger totally take over.

I got two of my friends who didn't mind fighting, to help me beat up both of the thieves separately. Instead of two against one, like when they stole my watch, it was three against one; us three against each one of them separately. My basketball Coach and I seemed to have communication problems after that incident. He told me how much I would have to do to rebuild his trust in me.

I had communication problems with my High School basketball coach, mostly because of his philosophy on basketball. His way of thinking was that all offense should flow through big postmen like himself standing about 6'-6. When I got in trouble for taking out my revenge on the thieves that stole my watch, things got even worse. I figured it was time for a change. Over the next two years through graduation, I would continue to work part-time jobs after school and summers, but my varsity high school basketball days were over.

Chapter II

"American Made Apparel"

"The Legacy – The Collapse"

"You won't have to worry about money, because you'll be rich and playing pro basketball one day". That's what Mr. Horton - my first basketball coach, and mentor - used to tell me. When Mr. Lorenzo Horton recently passed away, I was chosen to help eulogize him. Shortly before his death when Cancer and the advanced stages of Alzheimer's had ravaged his body to the point where his memory was no longer reliable, I visited him at his home. This was one of many visits. His wife Doris called out to him, "Lorenzo there is someone here to see you", as I walked into the room, his wife asked, "Do you know who it is?"

Much to my delight he responded, "Of course I know who he is, he's the basketball player." I considered for hours on end what I would say at the funeral. On the date of the funeral I was scheduled to be in New York City shopping SoHo, and Lower Manhattan. The trip was booked a month in advance, so I debated whether or not I should cancel my flight and go to New York at another time. I decided to pay extra and reschedule the return flight for an earlier time, so that I would have no conflict with the start time for the funeral.

What should I say about a man who had been so instrumental and encouraging in my life? Finally, it came to me. I decided to share the competitive brilliance, and creativity he exhibited as a coach, and how almost everyone who knew him admired his integrity. I told the story of how he coached his team to victory against my team. It was a very painful loss for me. Mr. Horton was my first basketball Coach, and his team was my former team. Our family moved to South Oak Cliff, and it was only seven blocks from where Mr. Horton lived.

Averaging 28 points a game, I was the leading scorer of all the schools we competed against. Mr. Horton had correctly surmised that his team would have to do something to curtail my scoring. Accordingly, Mr. Horton devised a plan within the confines of the rules and regulations that essentially won his team a hard-fought victory. What he did was brilliant, because he used all of his players including those who rarely played, to foul me every time I touched the ball, before I could shoot. This plan drastically limited the number of shots that I took, and consequently limited my teams overall scoring production, since I was only getting one free throw shot for a foul before the act of shooting, as opposed to two shots when in the act of shooting. He didn't cheat, he used the rules to his advantage.

My teams' coach - Mr. Sam Ferrell - was caught off guard and did not respond effectively. Our team's lack of a strategy to adapt to the opponent's tactic, cost us the victory. Although some would argue that the strategy Mr. Horton used was unethical. I disagree. It was crafty and bold, but not cheating. Mr. Horton was straight as an arrow, I never saw him take a drink or smoke, or say a curse word, in my whole life. As a child he used to take his youngest son Kenneth – who became my best friend - and me to Pro basketball games.

As an adult, he hosted me and my wife to Church with him and his wife, and Rotary Club meetings. Everyone I knew held him in the highest regards. After the game Mr. Horton and my former teammates were ecstatic about their victory. I was crushed to lose a game that way, but I had to pull myself together and be a good sport, the way Mr. Horton taught me. After the game I cried alligator tears from the agony of defeat, and my former teammates celebrated in the thrill of victory, yet we all shook hands and remained friends.

A loved one's funeral has always been a time for deep introspection of purpose, and relevance in my life. On my return flight from shopping in Lower Manhattan, when I knew what I would say in the funeral, I wondered how Mr. Horton would feel about my Black-Market shopping spree?

The decline of American made apparel fueled the sales of counterfeit, and Black-Market fashion products worldwide, and set the stage for hard working Americans who might otherwise be unemployed to make more than $10,000. a day in the Black Market. The Apparel and Footwear industry currently has annual retail sales of almost $400 Billion in the United States alone. 97% of this merchandise is imported, and factors heavily against the United States $222 Billion trade deficit with China. (According to the American Apparel and Footwear Association - AAFA, which is formerly known as the AAMA (American Apparel Manufacturers Association).

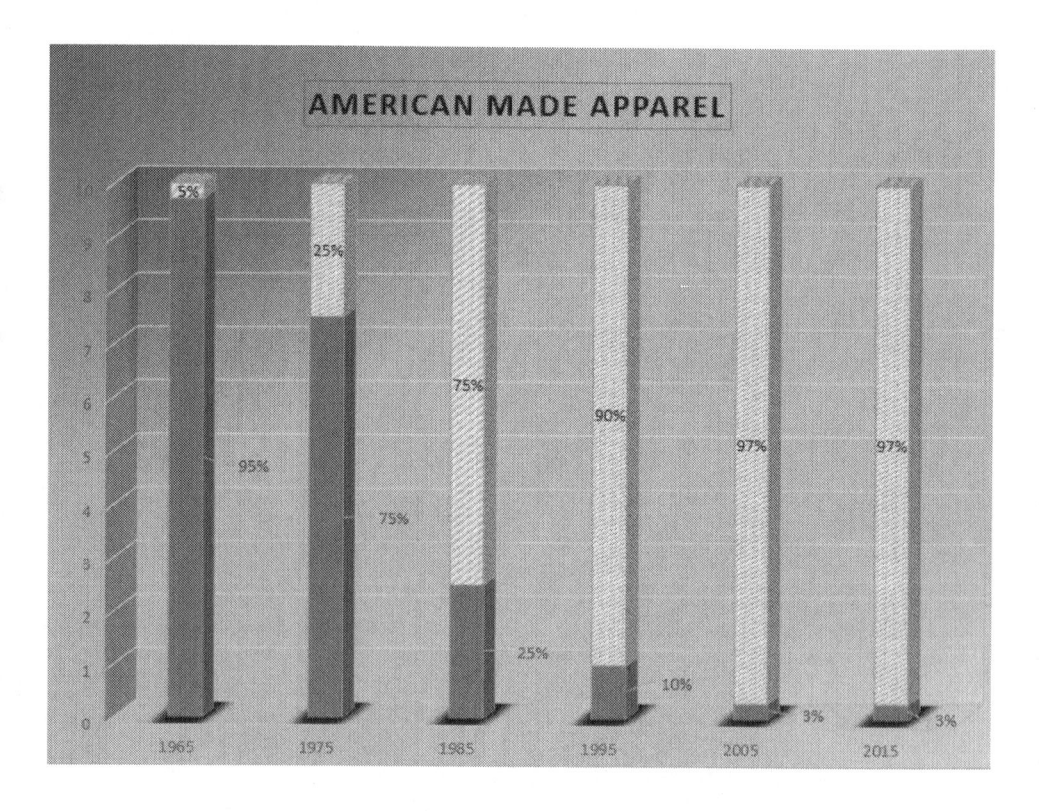

AMERICAN MADE APPAREL

Year	Made in America	Imported
1965	95%	5%
1975	75%	25%
1985	25%	75%
1995	10%	90%
2005	3%	97%
2015	3%	97%

Made in America=Solid*****Imported to America=Stripes

Chapter III

The Dallas International Apparel Mart

Because the 1.8 million sq. ft. Apparel Mart - demolished in 2006 - was the largest Apparel Mart in the world under one roof, it was very special. The collapse of the Dallas Apparel Mart had reverberations, and its demise speaks volumes about the failed state of U.S. production of apparel vs. what apparel we wear that is produced overseas (2% vs. 98%).

Built in 1964 The Dallas International Apparel Mart was the size of more than 36 football fields in total area, with beautiful restaurants adorned by towering cascaded stucco walls that stretched 5 stories to the solarium ceiling above, and water fountains that pierced the spacious ambiance 30 feet above the floor.

The Apparel Mart brought buyers and sellers together in a most luxurious and comfortable venue and was the economic engine of the Dallas Apparel Industry. The Dallas Apparel industry of the 1970's was second in the nation only to New York City. The Apparel Mart was also a venue for large civic, and social events in the Great Hall.

It was truly a magical place where many dreams came true, and many hearts were broken when the industry started to collapse. The customized showrooms were lavish, with mauve colored stucco walls, Areca palms, and soft plush shag carpet. So impressive was this building that the 1976 science fiction thriller movie "Logans Run" was partially filmed in the Great Hall of the Apparel Mart.

The Dallas International Apparel Mart – Great Hall. *Courtesy of Trammel Crow Holding LLC.*

The Dallas International Apparel Mart – Great Hall. *Courtesy of Trammel Crow Holding LLC.*

The Dallas International Apparel Mart – Great Hall, from the 3rd level.
Courtesy of Trammel Crow Holding LLC.

The Dallas International Apparel Mart – Great Hall; auditorium setup.
Courtesy of Trammel Crow Holding LLC.

The Dallas Apparel Mart – Great Hall, Private Suites with balcony. *Courtesy of Trammel Crow Holding LLC.*

The Dallas Apparel Mart — Great Hall; Dinner for President Lyndon Johnson.   *Courtesy of Trammel Crow Holding LLC.*

The Life and times of the Dallas Apparel Mart

Courtesy of Dallas Morning News

Usually, it's easy to spot a landmark in Dallas. In a city where old buildings were built in the 1970s, any truly vintage structures stand out. But one local landmark – recently set to close after almost 40 years – goes largely unnoticed. The Dallas Apparel Mart is an easy building to overlook. Located on Stemmons Freeway just northwest of downtown, the big beige box can't compete with the eye-catching architecture nearby, such as the Infomart, Anatole or that corporate headquarters of kitsch, the turreted Medieval Times. News last month that the wholesale building which soon shut down caused little stir except from the folks who work there. But its planned obsolescence is a milepost on the timeline of Dallas business. Every dog has its day. And in the 1960s, the dowdy– looking Apparel Mart was a stopping-off point for the so-called jet set that ruled international fashion and design. "People came from all over the world to that building" recalls Delores Lehr, who did public relations for the Dallas Market Center for years. "I can remember Oscar da LaRenta at shows there, and Bill Blass." You can add famed Hollywood designer Edith Head, Otto Kern, Diane von Furstenberg, Pierre Cardin and dozens of other designers to the list of dignitaries who have trooped through the Apparel Mart since it opened in 1964. By the late 1970s the weeklong seasonal shows were attracting more than 15,000 visitors. The building even starred in a big – budget Hollywood movie. Like Neiman Marcus, the Apparel Mart was a high-fashion outpost at a time when getting dressed up in Dallas meant putting on a clean shirt. Dallas developer Trammell Crow built the apparel Mart for $15 million. The entire complex, which covered two city blocks, took just 13 months to put up. They cut a bolt of suit fabric instead of ribbon at the grand opening. That night, Metropolitan opera star Rise

Stevens performed inside with the Dallas Symphony orchestra. The centerpiece of the apparel Mart was the one million-dollar Great Hall - a five story-high atrium-cum-performance hall where they held slick fashion shows, grand parties, posh luncheons in all such. Dallas architect Philip Henderson was on the design team Mr. Crow called in to create the Great Hall. They came up with a unique organic style with towering white plastered columns, trapezoidal skylights and three levels of curving balconies covering in terra-cotta mosaics. For good measure the later threw in three giant metallic snowflakes at the back. "The detractors called it polar bear modern." Mr. Henderson said this week. "We wanted to make it somewhat organic – something else then just rectangular." "It certainly was something for Dallas," he said. "At that time there was nothing like it." That's what the people who made the movie thought, too. In Logan's Run a 1976 science fiction flick, the Apparel Mart, the nearby Zale Building in the water gardens in Fort Worth were used to represent life in the 23rd century. The Apparel Mart likely won't make it there – there's already talk of tearing it down to build another Wal-Mart. "In the movie, they used the great Hall as the place they sent you when you were too old," said Mr. Henderson. That about sums things up.

Dallas, L.A. apparel marts bicker over which is No. 2

Courtesy of Dallas Morning News

Victor Costa would like to think that Dallas Apparel Mart is No. 1 at being No.2. But the Dallas designer of eveningwear can't ignore the fact that 20 percent of his taffetas are sold at the California Mart in Los Angeles. Their mart isn't anywhere near the best facility but in design and creativity, in fashion leadership, there's more on the West Coast," Costa says. "Now when we're talking about facilities, we are talking about marketing. In marketing the Dallas Apparel Mart is a monument to what is possible". For almost 20 years Dallas and Los Angeles apparel marts have fussed over who's on first when it comes to being second. Buyers manufacturers and designers using both say the facilities are opposites in strengths and weaknesses; Dallas is a sophisticated business first, high-volume selling machine; Los Angeles is a laid back come and go as you please place carrying the cachet of West Coast design talent, although not all prestigious California designers show their creations at the facility. There are a few statistics to prove that either trade center is better than the other but there are plenty of opinions. The April issue of Vogue offers a one sentence verdict, the Bible of the trendy set names Dallas Apparel Mart the country's biggest fashion industry Attraction outside New York. But Dallas designer Janet Barboglio, despite and admitted loyalty to her hometown believes the California Mart is on the verge of becoming tremendously viable because of recent efforts to organize wholesalers marketing efforts.

California sportswear maker Leon Max calls the Los Angeles Mart homier and complains that "the Dallas Mart is too hard to navigate. "But we see more traffic in a shorter time there than in New York or here" Max says. "I am very impressed with the professional level of business in the Dallas

Mart". The Marts similarities are few: Both are 19 years old. Both are owned by family companies. The Apparel Mart is just one of many holdings of developer Trammell Crow Company. The California Mart, and some adjacent real estate being held for expansion, is the only holding of the California Mart company, a limited partnership involving the sons of two lingerie manufacturers, their aunt and two-family friends. Both share the overall concept of offering thousands of lines in one, conveniently located building. And their differences are many:

California Mart showrooms are open year – round. Most Dallas rooms are open for special shows only. Each claims these aspects as strengths, though the California mart attempts to consolidate different wholesalers shows into special show weeks, as Dallas has, and Dallas is trying to persuade wholesalers to keep their showrooms open 365 days a year, as California has.

Donna Knox, vice president-marketing, soft goods leasing at the Apparel Mart, says "Dallas is more economically feasible for buyers. They can come in for three to five days and do what it takes weeks to do in New York. We have New York's great lines, we have California's sportswear, and they can get it all here. Bob Becker, California Mart marketing director counters my by pointing out the advantages of allowing buyers to shop at their convenience. He believes buyers may purchase more at the West Coast mart because they spend more time there making two or more trips to the Dallas-bound buyer's one.

Because neither records sales volume, some of the claims are impossible to substantiate. Dallas lacks a substantial manufacturing base. California's manufacturing base is not huge, but Costa says "if you took all the Dallas manufacturers out of the Dallas mart, it wouldn't even be felt. In California, the same thing would be noticed." The marts' staffs agree. The mirror– encased California Mart is in downtown Los Angeles, an area through which mart shuttle drivers warn visitors against strolling. The mart frequently is described as resembling an office building and it's cramped interior does little to change the impression. In Dallas, however, the Apparel Mart is a monolithic edifice adjacent to a freeway several miles from downtown. Walking there also is ill advised: the mart is surrounded by a tree-dotted parking lot but few sidewalks, and it is in the center of what is billed as the largest wholesale market center in the world. The mart's exterior is landscaped with raggedy climbing ivy, beds of recently planted golden pansies and artwork trucked here and there. Inside, tapestries, artifacts and sculptures are displayed. A cavernous meeting hall forms the business center of the building.

Access to the California building's mezzanine and patio area is unrestricted. To get into the Dallas Mart IDs are required. Although both mart's offer full selections of apparel lines, Dallas is known for its selection of missy dresses and better ready-to-wear, California for its junior items, swim and active wear. But Pam Roberts, fashion director of the California Mart, says there is a very, very small difference between merchandise available in the two centers. "Just about every New York line shows here," Ms. Roberts says, "and I know just about every New York line shows in

Dallas." Major California and Dallas lines show in both marts as well. The buyer – clientele differs along regional lines, too. Most apparel buyers shop in the mart closest to them. The Dallas Mart draws largely from the midwestern states, while the Los Angeles mart draws buyers from states west of the Rockies. Despite the ballyhoo about one mart or the other being predominant, few buyers shop both marts. With so much contradictory information wholesalers faced with two 2nd-place choices ignore the whole question and show at both or neither, opting instead to stick with No. 1, New York. "No majors (large department stores) regularly shop Dallas or L.A.," says Patty Cappalli, a California designer represented in New York, Dallas, Los Angeles and, elsewhere. "That's why we'll always keep showrooms in New York". Homi Patel, vice president of Hartmarx Corp's. M.Wylie division, agrees with Cappalli. "I don't think there is a No. 2. In common, both marts aspire to that. But it's really irrelevant to us," he says. "As long as New York is the strong national market it makes no difference" Patel says. "Dallas and California are basically regional, and it makes no difference to us who is No. 2 or 3 as long as they continue to draw their regional traffic." Even the marts public relations staffs, which vigorously support their facilities declared status, shy away from answering questions on the relevance of being the mart that tries harder. "I don't know if the number is important, if it matters" California's Becker says." But we are in the most innovative city. Trends develop here. And the mart is synonymous with the industry." "Well I don't know if being

No. 2 is important" Ms. Knox says. I'm pretty sure that all manufacturers care about is how many dollars they can book in Dallas."

The Dallas Apparel Mart was 1.8 million sq.ft. The L.A. Apparel Mart was 1 million sq.ft. The Great Hall in the Dallas Apparel Mart seated 4,000. The L.A. Fashion Theater seated 450. Parking spaces on premises; Dallas 9,200: L.A. 3,000.

There was nothing quite as glamorous, and festive as the last day of market, where you could see Calvin Klein walking down the corridor, flawlessly dressed in suit and tie, with two beautiful secretaries taking dictation on each side of him. This was a stark contrast to the first day of market where corridors were full, and there would be lines of buyers waiting to get into some of the showrooms. On the last day of market, wine and champagne flowed freely in show rooms all down the corridors, and there was always plenty of delicious food catered in for buyers and staff to enjoy. Also, on the last day of market, quite a few showroom salesmen would sale their samples at ridiculously low prices.

My involvement with the Apparel Mart came first in 1975, when I was a designer, with my own label of Mens High Fashion Sportswear (Grand Stand) and the Apparel Mart was at its peak. Amongst my most high-profile clients were the Dallas Cowboys, and a good number of other local celebrities. I also sold to several Mens Clothing stores in Downtown Dallas, and Houston.

In 1981 I was a buyer, and General Managing Partner of Downs and Walls Sporting Goods - A partnership with Dallas Cowboys Micheal Downs, and All-Pro Everson Walls. The first stages of decline had begun to show in the business activity at the Apparel Mart, during this period of time.

In the 60's and 70's ladies and men's specialty stores covered the Downtown Dallas landscape from east to west, in Deep Ellum on the east to Lamar St. on the west side of town.

Large Department Stores such as Sanger-Harris, Titches-Goettinger, and Dreyfus & Son, co-existed with smaller specialty stores like Colbert-Volk, Irby-Mayes, Reynolds-Penland, James K. Wilson, E.M. Khan, and a very small store on Akard St. that had really nice, and unique merchandise, named King Tailor. Before the giant mall shopping centers like North Park came in the late 60's, Dallas suburbs had strip shopping centers like Casa Linda, Wynnewood, and Big Town. There were many independent clothing retailers scattered around town, such as Roberts, Lester Melnicks, Margos LaMode, Marie Leavells, & Levines.

Apparel manufacturers, piece goods suppliers - fabric warehouses and stores - buttons, and zipper suppliers, large and small, were literally all over the city landscape.

Chapter IV

Working at The Neiman-Marcus Flagship Store

As an adult I have reminisced about how fortunate I was to represent Neiman-Marcus as one of the very few Downtown Delivery boys at 16 years of age. I was responsible for making deliveries of small packages of merchandise ordered over the phone to people who worked in the Downtown area.

In retrospect its clear to me that I was blessed to get to know an absolute genius in the retail, and fashion merchandising world. I can clearly remember my brief and rare encounters with Mr. Stanley. I always had the utmost of respect for him, even though I had no idea of his influence on the whole city of Dallas, and certainly not his influence on the entire world of High Fashion merchandizing.

His leadership skills will probably never be matched in fashion merchandising, nor will it ever be matched for civic contributions. It is most unlikely that history will permit such an achievement in our lifetime.

He is to the world of high fashion merchandising, what the whole dream team of Jordan, Magic, Byrd, Malone, etc. was to international Olympic Basketball.

Examples:

Mr. Stanley had foresight; In a **1966** speech at Indiana University, he predicted something he called "**phonovision**."

"The mass use of color phonovision will introduce a completely new dimension to remote buying and selling," he said in 1966. "Customers will be able to see the articles over the monitor that will interest them right in the comfort of their own living rooms." *Stanley Marcus*. Maybe Jeff Bezos (Amazon) took note.

Today, neimanmarcus.com has larger sales than any of their physical stores.

Mr. Stanley (Neiman-Marcus) was the first to produce weekly fashion shows.
Mr. Stanley(N-M) was the first to offer legendary his and hers gifts.
First to offer customer rewards program.
First American store to produce International Fortnights.

Neiman-Marcus IS the Gold Standard in retail merchandising. No one ever told me, and I had no idea that I could expect to see Hollywood movie stars shopping in the store on a regular basis. I was shocked to see King of the Cowboys, Movie Star, John Wayne shopping there. Lucky for me that John Wayne was one of the few movie stars I could recognize immediately.

However, there were many more Hollywood celebrities of smaller stature who would invariably cross my path in the store on a regular basis. Neiman-Marcus handled the Royal Wedding of Princess Grace Kelly of Monaco, and The White House Wedding of President Lyndon B. Johnson's daughter to name just a couple.

These were only a few of the many elite clients worldwide, who recognized that they could rightfully expect to find the very best quality clothing and fashion products in the world available at this store. Mr. Stanley followed a mandate from his predecessors - father and aunt - to find the best merchandise in the world. He carried out his mission.

His journeys carried him to some of the most remote areas of the world, such as India, where he discovered Shahtoosh, the rarest, and most expensive fabric in the world. This hand-woven fabric is said to make the finest cashmere appear inferior by comparison.

He promptly bought all of the Shahtoosh fabric available and brought it back to Dallas to be sewn into custom garments. The store advertised his and hers bath robes made of Shahtoosh in the Christmas catalog for $12,000. each. Of course, they sold out. Stanley Marcus: "I traveled the world and could buy anything I thought I could sell, and I had great enthusiasm that I could sell anything that I bought."

In the 60s and 70s many people including myself worked on 2 and 3 jobs to be able to buy things we wanted. As a sixteen-year old high school student, I worked three part time jobs to buy the 1968 Pontiac Firebird that I wanted so badly. Even though my car was a very nice one, it was a slightly used six cylinder with 1100 miles on the odometer. Because the value of a dollar was so great in 1969, I bought the car for only $2800. and my monthly payments were only $68.11.

One week after getting my new car, I was arrested for driving with no license. When a police officer pulled me over, he became really aggravated because I did not have a driver's license, but I did have my Neiman-Marcus employee identification card, which he mistakenly thought was a credit card.

He told me he was going to lock me up to teach my uppity ass a lesson, because of the new car, and what he thought was a N-M credit card. So, for three hours, I was incarcerated in a holding cell, until my parents came to pick me up. I had to park my new car until I could get a driver's license. My Father facilitated my Driver's License through a Black-Market connection that he hooked up two weeks later.

This was my first experience with the black market. We paid $100 to a man my father knew, and he took us to another man at the drivers' license testing facility. They gave me the standard driving test and made me two years older on my drivers' license, at eighteen years old instead of sixteen. I got the temporary license that day, and the permanent license came in the mail a few weeks later.

My part-time, after school, and summer job at Neiman-Marcus exposed me to many of the most talented, and polished merchandising, and salespeople in the country.

They were beautiful, and sophisticated people, always cheerful, and enthusiastic. I will never forget the stores top undercover Security Agent, Mr. Jackson. Tall slender about 6'2" 190lbs., well groomed Afro-American, always impeccably dressed in a custom fitted suit, necktie and white shirt.

Mr. Jackson's job was to keep the store safe from thieves, robbers, and anyone else who might try to illegally take advantage of Neiman-Marcus. One sunny autumn afternoon, which would have been a Saturday, I made the ill-advised choice to use my employee discount to buy merchandise in the store, for a friend that I barely knew. While I walked through the men's shoe department with my friend, he picked the shoes he wanted me to buy, and gave me the money.

Mr. Jackson surveyed the planned transaction from a stealth position. Before I returned to the shoe department later that evening, to execute our stupid plan to get my friend an employee's discount, Mr. Jackson called me to his office. He told me that he knew exactly what I had planned to do, and if I liked working there, it would be a good idea to never try that kind of stunt again. I promised him that I would not.

My duties included retrieving purchased merchandise from all of the departments for shipping when a customer requested, their purchases be shipped to a specific address. For people like me, who are intrigued by the art of fashion, the Neiman-Marcus flagship store was a wonderland, where you could find some of the worlds most unique and highest quality fashion products. I remember this one beautiful black dress that I retrieved from our ladies couture department. The fabric felt like cashmere, but it must have been Shahtoosh. **Shahtoosh is the most rare, and the most expensive fabric in the world, bar-none.**

As a sixteen-year-old, I knew nothing about the characteristics of vicuna, or shahtoosh fabrics. But as an adult with a lot more exposure and knowledge of fabrics, I now know that it had all the characteristics, of Shahtoosh. It was marshmallow soft, and smooth as butter, I had never felt anything quite like it before. The dress had a price tag of $3,200. in 1969, which equals about $22,000. today. I had felt the texture of the finest cashmere sold in Neimans-Marcus many times before, and the texture of this fabric was on another level. Much softer, and smoother, even buttery. The price of $3,200. in 1969 would be commensurate for a dress made of shahtoosh, and certainly much more than a dress made of cashmere, or vicuna. I have no way to verify at this late date that I was indeed, adoring the rarest, and most expensive fabric in the world, but it is very likely. However, it has dawned on me, as an adult that I was surrounded by the absolute most rare, and highest quality fashion products in the world, every day that I came to work.

There were exquisite Italian, and French made men's shirts both knit and woven, including Christian Dior that still today set the standards of class and style for men. The accessories were unique, very artistic, and clever, such as the watch I bought, which had a black spider web design on a platinum face - no numbers, just diagonal lines from the center of the web - with a rectangular gold-plated case, and black alligator band. The lines in the spider web were all diagonal, and not curved, which made it look more like a real spider web. The shape was just like a classic Cartier Tank watch.

There were very affordable, high quality men's suits. So much so, that even I could buy a couple of suits with my 25% discount for under $200. out of my part-time wages. However, the price could go astronomical on custom made Oxxford's in raw silk or, rare imported wool fabrics.

The Christmas season, and Fortnights at the Flagship store were the most magical times I remember from working there. "Amateurs imitate; artists steal." Stanley Marcus got the idea for Fortnight, expanded it and shaped it into a merchandising art form. One day in 1956, the Mr. Stanley was soaking up the sights of downtown Stockholm, Sweden. Suddenly, he saw something in a store window he liked very much: a colorful display of French merchandise.

The store itself was decorated in tricolors and had a French fashion show, as well as an imported French chef. Marcus talked to the Swedish store's management, learned that the French government had helped foot the bill, and soon flew to Paris to meet with officials of the Comité des Foires.

There, he promised the skeptical French a celebration on a grand scale that would benefit their industry and tourism if they would split the costs and help round up key spokesmen for the arts and economy of France. Marcus then held a press conference in Paris to announce his scheme and flew back to Dallas to convince local business and civic leaders to help him turn his new idea into a city-wide event.

He succeeded, and Time Magazine quickly dubbed him "The Man Who Sells Everything." The sights of Fortnight were never overbearing, subtle amber lights, sounds of light music in the background, and plenty of chatter from excited passing shoppers, and wonderful smells of terrific fragrances coming from the cosmetics department on the corner of Commerce, and Ervay.

This was always my favorite entrance to the store because the fragrances were synonymous with pretty women. Pretty women were always abundant in the cosmetics department, from the staff behind the counters, to the customers who frequented the store.

There were always a lot more people shopping in the store during the Christmas season and Fortnight. To this very day, Fortnight imitations are being staged in major department stores across the United States and in parts of Europe. "Fortnight is probably the most copied merchandising technique in America," said Stanley Marcus, who developed the concept in 1956 as a way to offset the slowdown that usually hits fall sales about two months before the Christmas rush. We also had more employees during Christmas and Fortnight, as seasonal employees joined the gift wrap and sales staff. It was easy to sense the excitement, and joy in the atmosphere.

For a sixteen-year-old who grew up watching Gunsmoke, and all the other cowboy movies, it was fascinating to see movie-superstar John Wayne - king of the cowboys - come into the store shopping with his entourage. At sixteen I was about 5'-11", and John Wayne looked like a 7-foot-tall man to me back then, even though he was really 6'-6".

I was only about 10 feet away from them, when I noticed John Wayne surrounded by his entourage of 5 or 6 men, who were all shorter than him. They approached the men's accessories showcases. He was wearing a light gray suit with a white shirt and dark necktie. I have many terrific memories about working for the best specialty store in the world. It may come as a surprise to many people who have only shopped at Neiman-

Marcus from a distance, and those who have not shopped there at all, that the very best foods available, were also sold in the store.

The strawberry preserves in the Epicure Shop was the absolute best thing anyone could ever possibly put on a warm buttered breakfast biscuit, and the Shrimp Newberg, and imported ice cream in the Zodiac restaurant on the mezzanine, all set the standard of best foods on earth.
There is however one memory that stands out far more than any in the big picture: While making a delivery for Neiman-Marcus to a Downtown office, I met Architect Mr. John Wesley Jones.

Mr. Jones office was right across the street from Neiman-Marcus, the office was directly above the top rival to Neiman-Marcus; Dreyfus & Son, also the store that Al Neiman joined, after the divorce with Carrie Marcus (the Aunt of Stanley Marcus, and Co-founder of the store). Al Neiman's partnership was bought out by the Marcus family.

Mr. Jones had placed an order by phone and requested delivery to his downtown office. As I entered the office, I noticed the drafting tables, T-squares, and triangles, and it became clear to me that it was an architectural firms' office. It was clear to Mr. Jones that I was fascinated with architecture, and we engaged in dialog about my career endeavors. When I told Mr. Jones about my interest in Architecture and wanting to compete in the Southwest Young Home Designers Competition at school, he volunteered to let me use his office, and equipment. He gave me a key so I could work on my project during the weekends.

After several weeks of working on the design and discussing the design criteria with Mr. Jones and his apprentice Paul, I began to think that I would have a much better floor plan, and design by changing the original design. One week before the deadline, I decided to pull the trigger. I tore up the original design and created a design that featured an Atrium in the center of a 3200sq.ft. home - 5 bdrm. 3 bath, 2 car garage, with triple entrances. In 1970, I Won 8th place in the Southwest Young Home Designers Competition via the Dallas Independent School District, with consultations from Architect, John Wesley Jones.

All of the contestants who won first place, through seventh place made elaborate artwork of their designs in 3-point perspectives (3-D drawing) . My 3-point perspective was well conceived, but not very elaborate, due to the lack of time left before the submission deadline.

Mr. Jones and I both were certain that the design concept was an overwhelming reason that my entry won an award at all, because there was such a contrast in the embellishment of the three-point perspectives (3-D drawing) drawn by the other winning contestants.

This seminal event bolstered my confidence tremendously, and encouraged me to pursue even higher goals, because of the level of collaboration I had with such accomplished professionals as Mr. Jones, and his assistant Paul. Over a course of months Mr. Jones and Paul continually encouraged me to pursue a degree in Architecture at the University of Texas at Arlington, where they were both alumni.

That encouragement, and my mother's persistent push for me to have a backup plan to fashion merchandising for a career, in no small terms lead to me winning a job at perhaps the most prestigious architectural firm in the country; The Architect of the Capitol, on Capitol Hill, Washington DC.

The highest quality was the ultimate goal in Mr. Stanley's merchandising philosophy. For most astute people in the apparel industry which would include my Aunt's and myself, the decline of quality products was evident in the mid 70's. Our sentiments about the decline of quality was echoed by Mr. Stanley in the mid 70's that several of the store's suppliers were failing quality test which previously were a cinch for them. (Ref. Quest for the Best by Stanley Marcus). My personal experience in the following story sheds some light on his observation. At some point during the early 70s I decided to try buying my underwear from Neiman-Marcus. I picked the typical all white cotton tee-shirt, and jockey shorts, which carried the Neiman-Marcus label. I was surprised at how long the underwear maintained its shape and elasticity through a multiple year time frame, and all the machine washes, and drying. During the late 70s and into the mid-80s I went back and bought more underwear from the men's accessories department at Neiman-Marcus trying to duplicate my previous results, to no avail.

Today what is sold as the equivalent of the 100% cotton underwear that I used to buy in 1973, would hardly maintain its original shape and elasticity through typical machine washes and drying for multiple months, let alone multiple years? Something happened to the quality in many apparel products during this period of time, from 1975 to 1985, and I don't think it ever recovered.

More than any singular person Mr. Stanley has promoted cultural exchange with the governments of France, Italy, Britain, Scandinavia, India, South America, Brazil, and Australia through the Fortnights which focused not only on the absolute best merchandise made in those countries but also, their best fashion designers, artist, writers, scholars, and the performing arts, ballet, opera, musicians etc. Year after year people would flock to the Fortnights to witness exhibits such as paintings by Picasso, and many totally unique crafts.

Mr. Stanley Marcus (April 20, 1905 – January 24, 2002), had a huge influence on the social fabric of the city that he loved, my hometown, Dallas, TX. The most outstanding thing about Stanley Marcus was, in addition to being the most talented merchant in history, he was sensitive to the fact that the overall social fabric of the city would be enhanced by elevating socio-economic opportunities for African Americans, and other minorities. He made it his business to address this dysfunction, and did not allow his wealth, and privileged Harvard education to make him insensitive to the big picture; the overall quality of life in Dallas, and our nation as a whole".

The late Stanley Marcus was an unsung hero in the Civil Rights movement of the 60's.   Not only did Mr. Stanley hire many African Americans at Neiman-Marcus, but he also encouraged all of the 5000 suppliers and vendors selling to his stores, to do the same. (Ref. "Minding The Store", pg. 370, The Memoir by Stanley Marcus).

On a cool crisp Saturday morning January 31, 1981, I took my wife Claudia - who was my fiancé at the time - to DFW Airport, for a flight to La Guardia Airport, NYC. As we approached her boarding gate, by pure happenstance, she was on the same flight with Mr. Stanley. I was thrilled to see him there waiting to board the flight. I had no doubt that it was indeed Mr. Stanley, impeccably dressed in a black beret, and black cashmere topcoat. I told Claudia "that's Stanley Marcus my former employer. I'm going to talk to him for a minute." I walked right up to him and introduced myself.

I said, "hi Mr. Stanley". "You probably don't remember me, but I used to work for you at the Flagship store years ago". Without hesitation he said "really, so what are you doing these days, where do you work?" I said, "I work for Xerox, in the facilities engineering group". His eyes lit up with surprise. "Oh really", he said. "I brought your boss to Dallas". He said

"Marv Robinson (an African American attorney) is your boss, right?" I said "yes, Marvin Robinson is my boss". At this revelation I am sure I looked surprised as well.

We laughed together for a second, and kind of said something to the effect of what a coincident. As I was about to ask exactly how that came about, he asked me what my duties were for Xerox. I explained that I designed HVAC systems for different business groups within the organization, when expansions, and/or renovations were planned. Before I could ask him another question, he asked me how I liked working for Xerox. I told him it was terrific, and that I couldn't be happier. He said that he personally recruited Marvin Robinson to enhance the social fabric of Dallas.

I realized how brilliant and aggressive he was about the quality of life in Dallas. Marvin Robinson's first job in Dallas was heading up a MESBIC (Minority Enterprise Small Business Investment Corporation) which had the sole purpose of providing funding for qualified minority people who had an interest in owning a small business in the mid 1970's. That is where I first met Marvin Robinson. Marvin was the Director of the MESBIC, and a recent Graduate from Howard University Law School in Washington DC, hailing from Selma Alabama.

I would have to be naïve to believe that he would be able to come into Dallas and spearhead a MESBIC without the able assistance from someone like Mr. Stanley. Mr. Stanley along with his associates the Zales, and Sam

Bloom took decisive actions to circumvent the threats that there would be mass civil disorder, or riots in the streets of Dallas similar to other major cities during the turbulent 60's. I believe he did it because he believed in his heart, it was the right thing to do.

When I started to work in the store in 1968, there were African Americans in almost all the departments. Stanley Marcus must be credited for being proactive, because he could have taken a much more conservative approach and hired just enough African Americans to say the store was an equal opportunity employer, the same as most business operations.

Instead he hired a tall, dark, and beautiful, full-time fashion model like Desiree Craig, who was frequently on the runway in the Zodiac Room, and store Security Chief Mr. Jackson, as well as Claude Holmes; Men's Accessories Salesman, and many others. All of the Black employees I remember at the Flagship store were always well dressed, and polished to detail, they also possessed impeccable character and represented the store with grace and dignity, the same as all sales personnel at the Flagship store.

Pictured above is the 1978 hooded jacket in slate blue cotton denim, and silver buttons, shoulder epaulettes with blue stars monogramed on them, that I designed and produced exclusively for the Dallas Cowboys Super Bowl XII Champions. These Jackets were made in the fall of 1977 before the playoffs, and Super Bowl XII, which is why there are no insignias of the Championship that followed a short time afterwards.

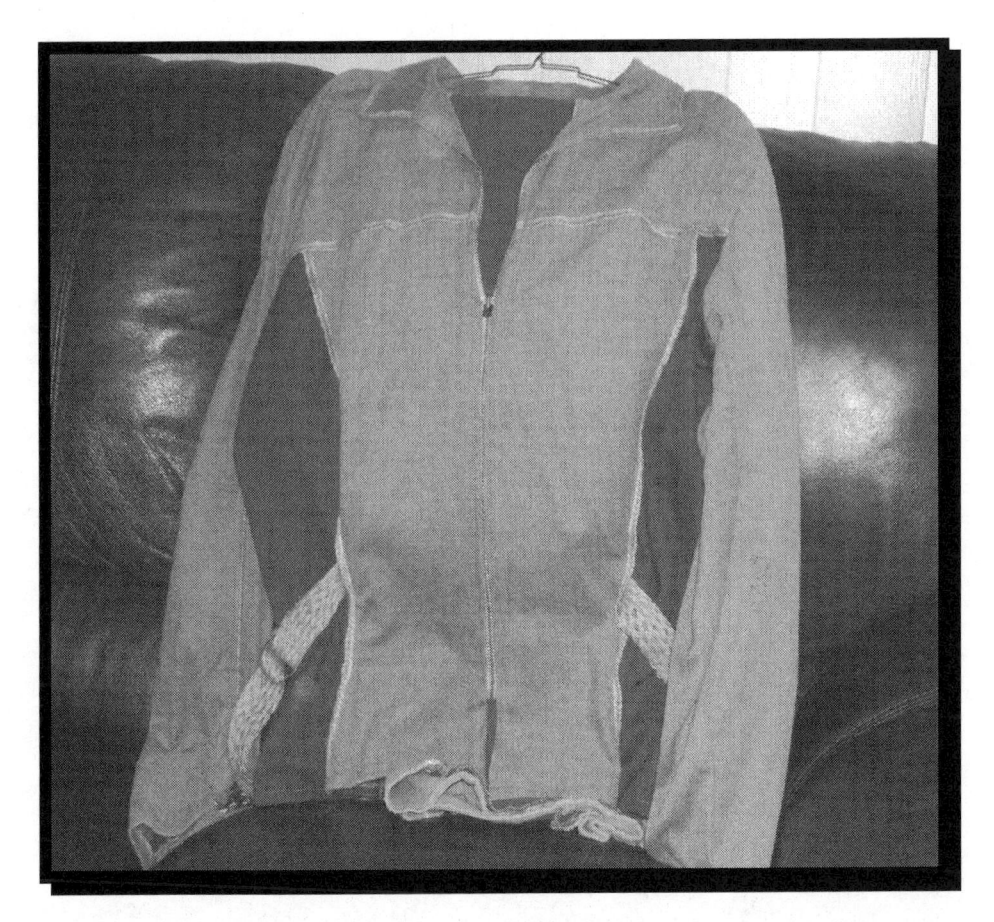

This is a two-tone cotton denim 2-piece suit, with burlap trim. This was my most successful design on the retail market, selling out of two Downtown stores, who proudly displayed it in their showcase windows. Legendary Hall Of Fame Cowboy Running Back, Tony Dorsett was the first person to purchase this design.

Celebrating a family reunion with Aunt Connie - 1998.

Left to right Stan Wooten, Connie Ravin, Kerwin Wooten(my son), Margaret Short - 2002.

1979 - I am wearing a two-tone cotton denim hooded jacket, with double chest pockets, and burlap trim. Legendary Cowboy Wide Receiver "Mr. Clutch" Drew Pearson was the first person to purchase this design.

Stan Wooten on Christmas Eve 2012, shopping at the Neiman-Marcus flagship store in Downtown Dallas.

Stan Wooten entering the BET Headquarters, and broadcast facilities in Washington DC, to do interview about a 1992 Educational Video produced by PCIA featuring 1992 NBA Rookie of the Year Larry Johnson who was also interviewed.

Xerox Corporation Black Caucus conference in Washington DC 1981.

Left to right; Marvin Robinson, (Xerox colleague), Leah Woodson, Stan Wooten.

Stan Wooten, at home in Houston apartment 1974.

1964 - Sixth grade Stan Wooten

The early 60s;Stan at nine years old with sister Vivian Wooten-fourteen-years-old.

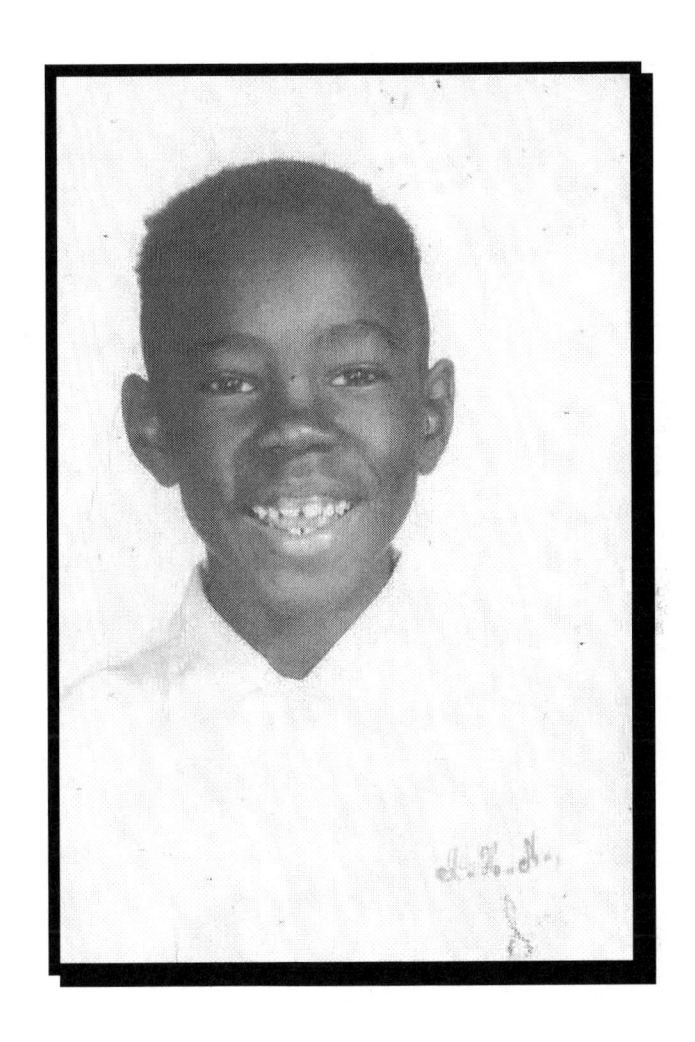

Innocence; Kindergarten at 5 years old.

Herbert Marcus Jr. Was a honorable man, and I'm so glad I got to know him. Herbert Jr. loved the arts much like his father, Herbert Sr. and his brother Stanley, and probably his whole family from all indications. Herbert Marcus Jr. was most definitely one of the people that I wish I could have spent more time with.

From 1998 until about 2000, I worked for a Consulting Engineering office in the Turtle Creek area of Dallas where Herbert Marcus Jr. operated a specialty signature coffee distributorship. After a surprise re-acquaintance on the parking lot of the office building, we shared, I pointed out that I used to work for the Neiman-Marcus flagship store downtown when he was there in the late 60s.

Herbert and I decided to get together later. He suggested I stop by his office when I got a chance, a few days later, I did. We talked for a while about my responsibilities at the engineering firm, and then a little about his business. He said, "you're not married, are you?" I replied, "no I'm not married anymore, I'm divorced". Shortly afterwards he told me that he had a favor to ask of me. I replied, "sure Herbert what is it?".

With no beating around the bush, or sugar coating he said "we, my wife and I have a dear friend who just recently divorced and we want to get her out, and I want you to join us, and accompany her at the symphony". Then he said, "she is the ex-wife of Major General Hugh Robinson". I didn't quite jump with joy. So he countered quickly", it's just a social event, we just want to help get her out". What a friend she had in

Herbert? Shouldn't we all be so lucky? I told him that I would think about it and let him know very soon. I knew very well who General Hugh Robinson was; Chairman and CEO of the Dallas Federal Reserve Bank, former Presidential cabinet member, living legend etc.

So how many guys do you know, who are not Super Star Athletes, or Movie Stars and are just really eager to date Michael Jordans ex-wife, or Tom Cruises ex-wife, or any woman who's had all the fame and fortune she could ever dream of. How exciting right? Of course, I had apprehensions about the fact that General Robinson was old enough to be my Dad, and his ex-wife, whom I had never seen before, was likely old enough to be my mother.

I don't think that mattered to Herbert, and it probably shouldn't have mattered that much for me either, because as he said," it was just a social event". At any rate I decided against it, and now regret that I wasn't more empathetic. It could have been a very pleasant experience, joining them all for an evening at the Dallas symphony.

Chapter V

The Beecham Sisters; Among Dallas' Finest Seamstresses

First and foremost, I have to say there is nothing quite like a holiday feast, and domino tournament at the homes of both, my Aunt Margaret, and Aunt Connie - now 91 and 97 years old respectively. They are both excellent cooks, and expert at table games, especially dominos, but also casino games.

They grew up in a time when most people sewed their own clothing instead of buying them ready made off the shelf. Their mother taught her five girls, Rosetta, Katherine, Oralee, Connie, and Margaret, how to cook, sew, and the basics of how to raise a family. This was the customary rites of passage for practically all young women growing up in the 1920s, and 1930s.

Left over fabric bags, that contained flour, sugar, and wheat, was used as fabric to make dresses and blouses. This was typical for poor families at that time in our nation's history. A needle, shears, and thread were the only tools used from the start, but in the late forties, pedal sewing machines became available.

On weekends, and holidays, Aunt Margaret was able to occasionally use a relative's pedal sewing machine, and that was the fascinating experience that clinched her passion for sewing. She began to spend a lot more time sewing clothes for herself, and her four sisters.

Following her passion, in the early sixties Aunt Margaret went to Industrial Sewing School, where she learned how to handle production of garments in high volume. After a short time, she was able to pass on her training to her sisters Connie, and Rosetta. After successfully completing the industrial sewing classes, Aunt Margaret began to work for Howard B. Wolf Inc.

Poised in the top echelons of ladies apparel makers in the industry, and employing over 700 people in several facilities throughout Texas, at their peak, Howard Wolf sold its fine ladies dresses to the big New York stores, such as Bloomingdales, Macys, Saks Fifth Avenue, and of course the hometown hero Neiman Marcus.

With Howard Wolf's demands for the absolute highest quality needle work in the industry, Aunt Margaret honed her skills, in an environment that challenged her development as a seamstress every day.

The 60's and 70's were a booming time for the fashion industry, and the three Beecham sisters were at the peak of their careers sewing for some of the top Designers in America, as well as custom garments for some of Dallas absolutely best dressed women. Rosetta, who was the oldest, started a sewing school in 1966 to train seamstresses for a career in a thriving garment production industry. Unfortunately, Aunt Rosetta died in 1972.

Aunt Margaret and Aunt Connie were very accomplished seamstresses who were starting to get recognition for their expertise and commitment to high quality. Margaret's leadership skills began to shine almost as much as her sewing skills and she became production supervisor for Howard Wolf, managing and supervising 25-30 seamstresses, in the production of high fashion ladies' apparel. Although Howard Wolf had sewing machine mechanics on staff, Margaret was known for doing light mechanical repairs on sewing machines, when the mechanics were too swamped with work all over the plant.

As time went on, and the demand for highly skilled seamstresses increased, Margaret, and Connie realized an opportunity to contract their sewing services out to several designers, and began their own contract sewing shops. They hired other seamstresses whom they met in the industry, and also top performers who completed their sister Rosetta's sewing school.

Although they trained, and developed the skills of many seamstresses, the turnover rate was rather high, because smaller sewing shops could not afford to pay all of the fringe benefits, to compete with many of the larger apparel manufacturers. Very often seamstresses would get the advanced training and leave for a job in a large factory that offered more fringe benefits.

For years the two sewing shops produced some of the most beautiful lace, velvet, and satin taffeta Holiday and Party, Ball Gowns ever sold in Neiman-Marcus, Saks Fifth Avenue, Bloomingdales, and Macy's. The Dallas Cowboys Superbowl Teams of 1976 and 78, wore jackets and other Hi-fashion sportswear produced by Connie and Margaret's sewing shops. The Dallas Ice Capades, and several high school bands purchased custom made uniforms from the sisters.

My label Grand Stand, which started in 1975 making, and selling Athletic Uniforms dressed many of the amateur adult and little league basketball, and baseball teams on the south side of Dallas. One of the closest held secrets for many years, was the fact that Aunt Margaret was chosen to sew exclusive designed dresses for Neiman-Marcus, using fabrics imported from Italy, Paris and Asia.

For the seamstresses there was not a great deal of glamour about the garment manufacturing business, except for the first samples. The High Fashion world is seasonal of course. The autumn and winter season - which includes the Christmas and New Year holidays - was always the dominate season. This was always a high priority in the business.

The first samples for the new season's designs were the fuel for the engine, especially first samples for Autumn/Winter. Of course, the absolute first eyes to see the new designs in full effect for each new season, would be the sample makers. You guessed it, my aunts and their crew.

Even though the hours were long, and the work was often grueling, my aunts made a comfortable living. My Aunt Margaret, along with her husband (Stanley Short) successfully raised five children Susan, Maryland, Stanley Jr., Patrick and David. The oldest girl was a real whiz kid. My cousin Susan Short was a straight A student through High school and was rewarded with numerous scholarships to many fine universities.

This was quite an accomplishment, which we all celebrate. Our family Attorney graduated from Vanderbilt Law School, in Nashville, TN, and is now a prominent attorney in that city. She serves on the board of directors for several civic organizations, including the Nashville Ballet, and has served on the board of regents for the State of Tennessee University system, her many awards, and achievements could fill this chapter.

Aunt Connie and her Husband successfully raised two children Mavis, and Leland, also Grandson Kanvin Ravin. Aunt Margaret, and Aunt Connie taught me a great deal about garment construction, such as using interface materials cut on the bias, as opposed to being cut parallel to the weave of the fabric. This diagonal cut made the interface material much more resilient.

They also referred me to others in the business for accessories, such as zippers, buttons, and thread to finish my designs. My prototypes (first Samples) were always impeccable because Aunt Margaret, or her sister Aunt Connie sewed them personally, with the same care and expertise that they put into the work they contracted for Victor Costa, which were sold in Neiman–Marcus.

Victor Costa was one of the most successful Ladies Wear designers in America. Mr. Costa is distinguished by his formal education at Pratt Institute, Brooklyn, New York, University of Houston, and École d'Chambre Syndicale de la Haute Couture, Paris, 1954-58, as well as his licensing agreement with Dior for the American market, and many awards in the Apparel industry. Victor Costa relocated to Dallas in the early 70s.

He became rich and famous due in large part to his ability to copy red carpet designs from the Academy Awards year after year. He became known by many as "the king of the copycats". His designs were made at a drastically reduced unit cost, as a result he was able to produce a much more affordable dress for his growing clientele.

Attention to detail, and meticulously superb needle work was what Aunt Margaret, and Aunt Connie were known for, and that would be just what I needed to get my designs showcased in the downtown store windows.

Shortly after I decided to join my aunts in the apparel industry, Aunt Margaret told me that there is a friend of hers who was very successful in the apparel manufacturing business. She said I needed to pay him a visit and introduce myself by letting him know that I was her nephew.

That man was George Scales who operated the largest Black owned apparel manufacturing operation in Dallas. He had a big operation in the Apparel Mart Industrial district, which employed over thirty people.

It is an honor to present my interview with Rev. George Scales below:

Rev. George Scales interview - 11/17/2017

Q: The Genesis; Please tell me how your story in the garment industry began?

Rev. Scales: "My foundation in the business came from ladies' wear manufacturer Nardis of Dallas, where I first started to work as a 19-year-old laborer and worked my way up from material (Fabric) handler. Later, I learned the basics of the apparel manufacturing business in terms of how to efficiently utilize the fabric for maximum yield and pattern matching for prints and plaids. These fundamentals were an absolute necessity for any growth or survival in the industry".

"I started Scales Cutting Service in 1969-2007 (38 years). We later added contract sewing services, and even later a ladies-wear manufacturing operation with my own designers, pattern graders, and outside wholesale marketing team. We also had a retail outlet store on Industrial Blvd. named House of George. The label we merchandised was Selah which targeted the southwest region which included Texas, Oklahoma, Arkansas, and Louisiana. Our ladies wear was specifically designed for the market we targeted".

Q: Were there other clients?

Rev. Scales: "Besides Nardis Of Dallas I had contracts with Larch Westway another major Dallas based ladies-wear manufacturer".

Q: How about financing for your operation?

Rev. Scales: "We had no financial backing. I never got bank loans from any of the institutions, we worked strictly off of our cash flow".

"After the Civil Rights movement stimulated opportunities for minority businesses, we saw buyers become more receptive to doing business with us in the 1970's. However, that did not last very long before other minorities such as Asians, Latinos and women started capitalizing on the hard-earned civil rights".

Q: How did the 1960's civil rights policies impact your business?

Rev. Scales: "The Affirmative Action and equal employment policies which opened the door to many jobs and business opportunities for Black people, began to decline as a vigorous white backlash spread across the country sweeping away much of the hard-earned gains of the late 1960's and 1970's".

"The absence of nationally organized Black leadership in the aftermath of the Dr. Martin Luther King, and Malcolm X. assassinations left the Black community more vulnerable and ill prepared for the backlash it experienced. In the late 1980's the surge in off-shore contract manufacturing in the apparel industry compounded the white backlash in our business".

Q: What was the major reason you are no longer in business?

Rev. Scales: "Two big reasons; I did not have adequate financing. In our business there would always be economic downturns, and seasonal fluctuations in revenues. Typically, the most successful businesses are the ones who have adequate financing to help them traverse the downturns and temporary financial problems".

"Secondly; Your competitors don't always play by the rules, and if your business operation is not properly financed you are a lot more vulnerable to attacks by competitors. In my case there was a larger competitor who disliked the fact that House of George (my manufacturing operation) was thriving.

Even though his market share was significantly bigger than mine, he chose to use his influence to cripple my relatively small market share. What he did was tell my biggest piece goods (fabric) supplier not to sell to me at all, or he would cancel a $20,000. order that he had just placed. My piece goods supplier told me he couldn't sell to me, for that reason".

I was fortunate to have worked with a few pioneers of the industry, my three aunts', and my fabric cutting contractor Hubert Johnson come to mind. I was not able to interview Hubert before writing this book, because he passed away shortly before I started the book project.

Hubert was a quintessential make it happen type of guy. He owned a large cutting service contracting operating which had ample space to grow. During the mid-70's Hubert teamed up with Mr. Iye, a Jamaican industry professional from NYC who had lots of manufacturing experience, and they made ladies apparel. They hired 10-15 seamstresses, and they worked in Hubert's building. I never knew much about their label, or where their products were sold.

Rev. George Scales shared a story about Hubert that I never knew. He said that Hubert helped him survive in the industry during the early years when they were both fairly new independent contractors. Hubert told George to move in with him until he could work his way out of a serious tax problem, he found himself in. I was so proud of Hubert's benevolence even though George and Hubert were competitors so to speak.

Chapter VI

Taking the Grand Stand Label from sketch pad to the store front window

The experience of taking a line of Hi Fashion Sportswear from a sketch pad to a showcase in a downtown storefront window, is a euphoria that I wish everyone could experience at least once in their life. The thrill of actually seeing your designs on the runway of a successfully coordinated fashion show, and in the Dallas Apparel Mart Showroom, is unforgettable.

Taking a product from the sketch pad to the retailer's display window was no simple task, especially for an inexperienced designer making a debut in the marketplace. The confidence that I could become a fashion designer was cultivated from many awards, and achievements starting at 9 years old.

The school's trophy cases would display my talents as a sculpturer, painter, and portrait artist. At nine and ten years old, I would draw very good pencil portraits of President Kennedy. To this day my former classmates still rave about those portraits.

Recognizing that I had talent for art, my mother arranged for me to get advanced training in summer school classes at the Dallas Museum of Art. I sincerely believe those classes helped develop my appreciation for the art of fashion. Every child in the United States who has the least bit of interest in art, should be fortunate enough to visit the terrific art museums throughout our country. Children also need well versed and enthusiastic ambassadors for the arts to help stimulate their interest. From these endeavors we become, a more creative, and productive society.

What I lacked in experience I made up for in hustle. This meant getting as many experienced industry professionals as possible on my team of consultants, and contractors. My task was made much easier, due to the fact that I had family members who were established in the garment making business.

However, that does not mean I never met resistance from my aunts about some of my designs and business decisions. To the contrary, I vividly remember the both of them complaining "that boy goes home and dreams up all kind of nightmares to sew". They forced me to think about practical, functional, and cost-effective designs, and things that a good designer should always consider.

They explained how interfacing material would be more resilient when cut on the bias (diagonal). I always listened carefully because I respected their opinions, and I knew they had my best interest at heart. I was determined to meet the demands of the marketplace, and team uniforms were a definite need. There were many amateur teams on the south side, both youth and adult which bought teams uniforms from me. I personally knew most of them. I pursued their business, and got it, producing mostly traditional baseball, and basketball uniforms, for several of the Comets little league teams of the Salvation Army. The jackets for the Cowboys Superbowl X, and XII, all of the custom garments for the Cowboy Superstars, everything I ever designed for my "Grand Stand" label, would have probably never happened without the support from Aunt Margaret and Aunt Connie.

During my senior year in high school I designed four, or five outfits including two leather and suede suits that I had made by a custom leather craftsman. It was during this timeframe when my Aunt Margaret came into the picture.

My mother told me that nobody was better than her at sewing anything. I went to her to discuss my designs, and she was so gracious about helping me get my designs just the way I wanted them. Because of her challenging me to pick the right type of fabrics that were ideal, and teaching me to cut my own patterns, I got an introduction to the product development aspect of the apparel design business. This was a plus because of the arduous task in getting a preferable fit from a garment. This was usually a very time-consuming challenge.

My patience was tested, and pushed to the limits time, and time again during the pattern making of the "One Suit" jumpsuits. These jumpsuits were my very first designs sold from a showroom in the Dallas International Apparel Mart. The showrooms in the Apparel Mart were leased by not only big-name labels (manufacturers), but also Manufacturers Representatives. Manufacturers' Representatives carried garments that were produced by many smaller independent manufacturers such as my Grand Stand label. Their mode of operation was to get the newest, hottest, styles that appealed to their varying clientele. Understanding this dynamic, I was able to present my prototype (first samples) which proved to be top quality and negotiate a mutually good commission for selling my garments, along with the many others they were already carrying.

Although the "One Suits" looked great when you were standing, they could be a little uncomfortable when setting. For this very reason my next designs for the jumpsuits featured a heavy nylon ribbed knit elastic waistband, with matching collar, wrist cuff in dark royal blue, accenting cobalt blue denim fabric for the body of the jumpsuit. Cowboys All-Pro receiver Drew Pearson was the first to purchase this design.

Because there was a thriving apparel manufacturing industry in Dallas at the time, good pattern makers, and good pattern graders, were not hard to find, if you knew where to look. Of course, the process of finding very talented professionals was made much easier for me because of my family ties. My Aunts directed me to some of the most talented people in the business.

My designs were bold, fresh, and edgy, always using buttons, zippers, and thread as part of the design, as opposed to being simple accoutrements. Some of these unique designs used raw materials such as burlap on denim.

There is no doubt in my mind that my fascination with art influenced my designs. The fact that I did well at sculpture, paintings, etching, and drawing portraits to the point of being showcased in the school's trophy cases through Elementary and Middle school most certainly enhanced my confidence. I believe that I had a virtually instinctive sense of symmetry, and color coordination. However, my summers spent studying Art at the Dallas Museum of Art was a catalyst to making good designs come alive.

Without a real fascination for the industry, and a little talent for art, I don't believe I would have had the confidence, vision or patience to see such a formidable endeavor through to fruition at twenty-two years old. There were two other extraneous factors that I must credit: I was surrounded by family members, and friends, as well as neighbors who loved high fashion apparel.

Looking good had a pretty high priority where I came from, and the right clothing did the trick for my family. The passion for fashion apparently ran in my bloodline. My father's temporary loss of control perhaps best evidenced this fact. Because Daddy as a 22-year-old new parent, once spent the family's monthly rent money on a fancy shirt. My mom said that Dad apologized to her, and felt very bad about it, but said he just had to have that shirt. Oh, that passion!! After my Mom and Aunt Rosie (Dad's sister) tag teamed him, he never pulled that stunt again. Last but certainly not least the streets of South Dallas, and Oak Cliff in the 60's and 70's had an abundance of swagger and style.

There was at least one R & B Show Band wearing outfits that carried my Grand Stand Label, as one of the Downtown Men's Retail Store Owners told me about. The Just-In Men's store had proudly put my blue denim and burlap trim 2-piece designs on display in their window and got very good sales as a result. Even though I believed my designs stood on their own, what could be better than having a superstar Pro Athlete wear your newest designs. Gaining access to professional athletes who were Dallas natives came easier for me, because once upon a time, I was considered one of the best basketball players in Dallas public schools, and among the best dressed.

As a sophomore in high school, my two most favorite suits, was my Neiman-Marcus light-gray pin-striped wool, two-button double breasted suit; and the camel colored wool gabardine, with bronze window-pane plaid Edwardian six-button double-breasted suit, which I bought in the boys clothing department at Neiman-Marcus. I found a superb Italian silk, Christian Dior shirt in a peach color for the light gray pin stripe suit, at Neiman-Marcus, it was on sale, and with my employee discount it was an even better purchase for me. For my camel colored windowpane plaid suit, I bought a raw silk, rust colored Schiaparelli shirt from Irby-Mayes which was across the street from Neiman-Marcus.

I typically bought a color coordinated silk pocket square to accent the suit and shirt with panache. My favorite shoes were my brown genuine alligator penny-loafers from Dreyfus & Son (a Wolf Brothers store) and alligator Foot Joys form National Shoe store on Commerce St., with matching alligator belts. I had three pair of alligator shoes. In the late 60's we would take our gator shoes to be glazed – not shined – at a little shoe repair and shine shop at the corner of Main and St. Paul streets, across the street from Titches department store. The glaze would make alligator shoes shine like glass. There was nothing like it. Most shoe repair shops nowadays know little to nothing about a glaze process.

Tom Ford is the current hottest new designer in the world of high fashion. He is the person credited for being most responsible for turning around the Gucci brand from falling off the cliff through the 1990s into the last decade. In response to the question of why he wanted to go to Europe and work for Gucci – he was quoted as saying "many people in this country look down on high fashion, as though it's a bad thing, whereas it's appreciated in Paris."

I am virtually sure that my passion for fashion irritated the hell out of many people, who did not have the heart to tell me. Even though I was one of the best dressed boys in Dallas Public Schools, my wardrobe was no match for my good friend, Lil Tim Jackson. He was probably the best dressed boy in Dallas Public Schools, of all-times.

Beginning in 1970 jeans, and much more casual attire started to dominate the fashion scene. Suits, sports coats, and blazers faded from the school campus, and/or school events. Alligator shoes, Banana Skin slacks, were virtually a thing of the past for students. Because of the fashion buying patterns in the 60s thru the early-70s in contrast to the later years, the best dressed boys in our public schools would have come thru this time frame of the 60s thru the early-70s.

In 1973 with the "Oil Crisis", and OPEC Oil embargo the value of a dollar took a long slow nosedive that cripple purchasing power for two decades – well into the 90's. This is why I believe we saw the best dressed boy students in the late 60s or early 70s. Lil Tim, as everybody called him, was about 5'-5" tall, 100lbs. as a senior in high school, and adopted the name "2 Short" after he became the personal Tailor for Ed "Too Tall" Jones of the Dallas Cowboys.

Tim bought vanity personalized license plates that read "2 SHORT" and put them on his new Lincoln Town Car. This was another Harvey Martin production. Lil Tim, and Harvey Martin were classmates since Junior High School, and Harvey introduced Tim to "Too Tall". Lil Tim, like me became a Mens Hi-Fashion Apparel designer. However, unlike me, Tim was a tailor who actually sewed his designs.

He was totally obsessed with high fashion apparel. He had no competing interest like sports and was known to brag about his extensive wardrobe. "I can go two months before I repeat" he would say. This meant for two whole months he could wear the best Banana Skins (wool gabardine slacks), suede front sweaters, Schiaparelli silk shirts, really nice wool suits, fine calf skin Bally shoes, and Alligator Foot Joy shoes, without wearing the same thing.

High fashion apparel was Lil Tim's thing, so he kept score. This was his game he seemed to think, and nobody was going to cheat him out of his title. When Lil Tim saw a guy wearing a real nice outfit, that he had noticed him wear before, he would say "nice outfit but, you're repeating ain't you". Nobody doubted that Lil Tim was the best dressed boy; however, his arrogance made a lot of enemies.

There was no counterfeit, or black-market clothing to be found like there is today. When you saw the well dressed guys wearing golf slacks like Sansabelts, or 100% worsted wool gabardine slacks that we called Banana Skins which came in four or five beautiful colors, you knew beyond any shadow of a doubt that you were seeing the best, of the best.

There was no mistaking when you saw Banana Skins, because the avocado green, rust brown, wheat gold, and slate blue colors were so unique. They could only be found at Irby-Mayes Mens Store (Ervay and Commerce Streets, directly across the street from Neiman-Marcus), and were very well made, also very expensive, about $75. a pair in 1968 (which would convert to over $500. in 2019)

In the late 60s and early 70s, High School star athletes from the south side had great fashion sense, and panache; that's what a lot of people call swag today. The State Fair, R&B concerts, big High School, and College football or basketball games were a showcase for the best outfits in Dallas.

I can still remember the State Fair 1969, when one of my best friends, Richard Harris, who was one the best all-around athletes in Dallas High schools at the time (football, basketball, and track with a 42 vertical jump); Richard was wearing a short sleeve lightweight wool, salt and pepper Jump Suit, that looked like it was tailor made for his 6'-2" 220lb frame. He topped it off with a really nice wheat colored straw fedora hat.

Nobody else that I knew, had a jumpsuit like his. Richard's jumpsuit was an inspiration for my 1976 design (eight years later) shown in a photo on page 149. Micheal Gilyard was no doubt the best all around athlete in Dallas Public Schools at that time (football, basketball, baseball, and track). Michael Gilyard was an honor student at Lincoln High School, and went on to Stanford University, becoming freshman of the year playing quarterback.

Michael was one of my best friends also. When he came home from Stanford University, we hung out a lot, so I got a chance to see his wardrobe up close. He had excellent fashion sense and wore some of the best leather and suede jackets in town, with matching suede caps. Charles "Duckeye" Harris, one of the best pure shooters to ever play basketball in Dallas, wore the notorious Jaguar hat, from Dreyfus and Sons. Kenneth Brigham, and his cousin Hubert Green, both close friends of mine since elementary school at N.W. Harlee; were both very good athletes with a lot of class. I still remember they both wore beautiful full length maxi top grain calf leather coats in 1969.

Burnis McFarlan, and Rufus Shaw both now deceased, were always impeccably dressed at big events like R & B concerts, such as The Temptations, or Stevie Wonder etc. Their images are seared into my memory forever, as I took note of their buttery smooth lambskin leather jackets and smooth calf skin Bally, or alligator shoes. I took my cues about fashion from these guys. They were all older than me, and the highest profile athletes in Dallas high schools at the time.

I found out much later in life that you could tell a lot about where a guy was raised, by the style hat he wore. In major cities around the country there are common hats that have gained a lot of popularity.

In the 60's and early 70's, there was a wool felt Fedora hat called the Jaguar. The Jaguar hat was sold at Dreyfuss & Son (a Wolff Brothers store) in Dallas. This hat which looks very similar to a wool felt Borsalino fedora, was also popular in St. Louis, and Chicago, as well as Washington DC, and New York. The Jaguar was the progenitor of the one and three-quarter inch (short to medium) brimmed felt Fedora, that has resurged on the urban fashion scene over the last twenty years.

When I called on my former teammates and NBA players, San Antonio Spurs, Ken "Grasshopper" Smith, and Portland Trailblazer, Ira Terrell (I.T.), and Dallas Cowboys Harvey Martin to model my designs, they were all to happy to do the favor, free of charge. For certain I had no grand illusions of becoming the next Da Vinci or Calvin Klein. However, I knew I had talent and good taste, and if I applied myself to a task, and worked hard at it, I could expect a very good outcome.

Pettis Norman was not only a NFL star Tight End for the Dallas Cowboys 1962, through 1973; he was one of the most successful businessmen in Dallas, and one of my best Clients. When I visited Pettis at his office on R.L. Thornton Freeway, to show him my designs, it was a hit right from the start. He really liked the design, so the next question was the fabric, and color.

I showed him my fabric swatches, and he decided on a Canary yellow, cotton pique fabric, with accented caramel colored needlework with wooden buttons, and belt buckle. Pettis told me later that he wore that jumpsuit to a high-profile Golf Tournament and got an abundance of compliments on it. To have my work admired, and appreciated by a very satisfied customer, was music to my ears as a designer.

I attempted to sell to larger chain stores such as Sanger-Harris in Dallas, Foleys and Joskes in Houston, all of which have since been acquired by the Macys Chain. There was a Mens sportswear buyer at the Foleys department store in Houston that, I knew by the name of Butch Nelson. Butch was a good friend of my in-laws, and was raised in Singing Hills, just blocks away from my in-laws' home. I thought I might be able to get a break with Butch and land an order. I got in touch with Butchs' sister Ava to get his personal phone number and gave him a call to set up an appointment.

I flew to Houston shortly after the call and met with Butch, only to be told that he was, just like other buyers in the chain, required to verify a 9 month to 18-month track record of on time deliveries for all new manufacturers. Butch also told me the same thing that I had been told before, by buyers at Sanger-Harris Dallas, that synthetic blends were not allowed.

On some of my One Suit designs I used cotton/polyester blended material, and that material choice disqualified them for these stores. Subsequently I was told that the designs looked terrific, but they just could not buy synthetic fabrics. For this reason, my Grand Stand label had to be sold to smaller urban men's stores, which were called Ethnic Stores in the industry.

My Aunts had sewing contracts with some of the top designers in the business, and a piece goods rate that was commensurate with their highly skilled craft. For this reason, my typical production runs of 250, to 400 units a month would have created a strain on their production capabilities with regard to their bigger and much more reliable clientele.

The plan was that I would have them sew my first samples, and another sewing contractor sew the production runs at a much lower piece goods rate. There would be a drop off in quality, which we expected, but we did not expect a very visible lag in quality. When a new manufacturing operation like mine was launched on a shoestring budget, every single day was important.

The goal of building a solid tract record for delivery was at stake each day. The worst thing that could happen was for there to be an interruption in the carefully planned sequence of events, in the manufacturing process. That is exactly what happened to my sewing contractor who, put my order of 300 units on the back burner, and prioritized a larger order for 1500 pieces, over my order, even though my order came in first.

First come, first served is usually the rule recognized by most of the industry. However, money talks and almost everybody in the Apparel manufacturing business wanted their products sewn yesterday. I have no idea, what kind of incentive Roxy, my sewing contractor was given. People are never too eager to share details like that. It was clear to see that she and her crew had a lot more work in her shop than when they started working on my order. My order was put on the side as Roxy and her crew worked on the bigger order.

Realizing what was happening I pulled my order and took the work back to my Aunts shops. Having to pull the order caused a late delivery and created lingering operational problems for my under financed and fragile new manufacturing organization.

Chapter VII

Rock Stars Influence on the Fashion World

Rock Stars had a big influence on fashion in the early 70s. The Woodstock concert was just wrapping up and the movie made of the concert was showing all across the country. The Eternally Hip Sly Stone, Jimmie Hendrix, Led Zepplein, Rolling Stones, Santana, and far too many more to name were blazing the charts and setting social discourse. The fashion world was swept up in the winds of change, as flower power shirts, and low-rise bell bottom pants dominated the apparel industry.

Fashion trends fortunately do not always follow celebrities lead. I am slightly embarrassed to say that I bought Sly Stones Woodstock long fringed shirt at The Gazebo in 1970, and proudly wore it to school one day along with custom made snow boots. This was the equivalent of the Michael Jackson "silver sequin glove". But Sly Stone opening up the Woodstock festival in something so unique as this fringed shirt was too tempting for me to resist. Sly Stone was the epitome of All-American cool for me. So, I bought the hat, the shirt, and the boots. When I ran into Savoy Young; a fine vivacious cheerleader on the stairway at school, immediately upon seeing me she literally cracked her side laughing. She was kind of square anyway, and I don't think she knew anything about the Woodstock music festival. Nobody else said a thing besides Savoy, but Savoy was right, I looked stupid wearing that to school even though it was 1970. I never tried that stunt again.

I remember that feeling of getting off track in cutting edge high fashion experiments. Even though nobody told me anything about my Sly Stone outfit, except that square ass cheerleader Savoy Young, who couldn't stop laughing long enough to say a word. I kind of felt like something was wrong.

High Fashion Designers live on the edge and are risk takers by nature. What we run the risk of doing is looking stupid if the design doesn't work the way we thought it would. One of my favorite drawings that I made in 1985 for my first book published in 1987, sums up my feelings. I share it below:

James "Bug" Baker could often be found dressed like Bootsy Collins at night clubs in the late 70's and had to almost fight his way out of the club, from guys dissing him. The Washington DC Bootsy Collins look-a-like had his act together. He was the Rhinestone Rock Star on the subway, and everybody knew it. He was just as Fly as Bootsy, and if you started to laugh at him, you would feel a little square, because the brother was cool.

Thank goodness no one wanted to copy George Clinton aka "Dr. Funkenstein". The influence that current Superstar entertainers have on fashion is still huge. Lady Ga Ga, Mary J Blige, Katy Perry, and Beyonce, are all very fashion savvy ladies that express themselves differently through their unique styles.

Bruno Mars is carving out his own niche in both the music world, and fashion world with his signature old school fedoras, and classic attire. I think Bruno Mars has good fashion sense.

Another good example of influence on the fashion world is when Jay-Z almost single-handedly escalated the Ray-Ban Wayfarer sunglasses as a top fashion accessory, worldwide. That was amazing to watch. It's no coincidence that Rihanna has advertised exclusively for Gucci, or that Madonna advertised a $5,000. Louis Vuitton purse in Vogue magazine. Advertisers recognize the celebrity influence on the fashion world.

The 70s were precarious times for youngsters, because rebellion against almost everything that was traditional became the order of the day.

This rebellion against traditional trends generated an abundance of creativity in high fashion, yet along with it came eccentrics and impracticality, like platform soled shoes.

Maybe it came from all the marijuana in the air we breathed during the early 70s, but for some reason quite a few people lost their bearing. My good friend Lil Tim was one of the people who definitely lost his bearing in the early 70s'. Lil Tim created some of the most eccentric designs that I can ever recall seeing and changed his name to T.R. St. Whitnauer to top off the eccentrics.

For most people like myself, who had witnessed Tim as a very neat, traditional fashion savvy young man in the late 60s, all we could do was scratch our heads, and wonder what happened, when we looked at his eccentric designs.

I consider myself fortunate to have been a big fan of Gentlemen's Quarterly (GQ) Magazine during the early seventies. I honestly believe this magazine helped me stay focused on mainstream high fashion. GQ in the early 70s pushed the fashion envelope enough to present a good range of creativity without going to extremes. We 18-year olds in the early 70s were somewhat bored with traditional fashion. Even though traditional men's fashions were represented in GQ, there were exciting new twist to them, such as untraditional colors, and corsage buttoners on the jacket lapel.

Recently I have been hearing the term "Fly". I even saw an e-mail advertisement from Nordstrom Department store using the term in their headline. The term was born out of the 1972 hit movie Super Fly. About a Harlem, NY drug dealer who was always dressed sharp with swag to spare.

His new Cadillac Eldorado car was even customized Pimp style. The movie was so successful that the term "Fly" would supplant Pimp style, swag, panache, elegant, excellent new hairdo, or just well dressed. The term "Fly" is commonly used in urban vernacular and is a typical lyric in Hip-Hop, Pop, and Soul/R&B music today over forty years after its birth. This term underscores the powerful influence of the 60's and 70's which this book salutes.

Chapter VIII

Pro Athletes Influence on the Fashion World

Over the 1978 New Year's holiday weekend my lady and I, met up with Dallas Cowboys All-Pro defensive ends Harvey Martin and Ed "Too Tall" Jones at the Americana night club on upper Greenville Avenue. The Americana was one of, if not the most elite night club(s) in Dallas (1978). This brand new hexagonal shaped night club was designed and built for the express purpose it served, as opposed to many night clubs which occupy buildings that were originally built for a different occupancy and later renovated to be used as a night club.

The weather outside was very cold, and there was an ice storm forecasted for that night. Harvey and Too Tall were a sight for sore eyes to see, wearing beautiful full-length silver fox fur coats that had to weigh 150lbs each.

Carrying his coat in the club, Harvey handed it to me and said "Stanley, feel how heavy this thing is, here hold it". He wasn't joking, it felt like 150lbs.. At 6'-5" and 6'-9", they were hard to miss, and even harder to miss wearing those stunningly luxurious full-length fur coats. In our society nobody but a few movies stars, Hip-Hop/Rock Stars, and maybe the President gets so much attention, and nobody pulls off high fashion like pro athletes.

There is perhaps no better example of a super-star pro athletes influence on the fashion world than when Michael Jordan decided to wear over-sized Chicago Bulls basketball trunks, to cover his sky-blue North Carolina Tar Heels trunks that he always wore under his uniform in 1987-88. Not only did the whole NBA soon follow suit, breaking a tradition of 40 years, but so did colleges, high schools, and even elementary schools.

This fashion trend was not only dominant on the basketball courts across the nation, it became sportswear. Young men began to wear the oversized longer shorts on the streets all over the country. This fashion trend has been running for over twenty-five years now and appears to still be going strong. Just like many other American fashion trends, oversized shorts have gone global, and you see them all over the world.

NBA on TNT television announcer, Kenny Smith who is also a former NBA star, wore peak lapel, single breast suits in 2002. The likes of which had not been prominent on the fashion scene in twenty-five years. There was nothing totally new about the design, because fashion is cyclical, and the time for this peak lapel single breast suit was due for resurgence. Seventeen years later the suit is still a very hot fashion item, even after such a long twenty-five-year hiatus. The hottest new designer on the market Tom Ford (who is credited for bringing the Gucci brand back to prominence over the last fifteen years), has made men's peak lapel suits, and blazers the stars of his new line-up. Calvin Klein, Hugo Boss, and others have all followed suit even more than a decade after Kenny Smith started the resurgence.

To their credit Sean Combs (Sean John), Russell Simmons (Phat Farm), and FuBu, recognized the strength of the trend almost two decades ago and sort of capitalized on the opportunity. There is no doubt that Kenny Smiths high profile as a TV announcer and former NBA star influenced this men's fashion trend. March 2010 the best basketball player on the planet at that time; Kobe Bryant appeared on the cover of GQ men's magazine wearing a dark grey, peak lapel, single breast suit. The suit that Kobe was wearing is virtually identical to a suit that I bought at Neiman Marcus in 1980 (shown in photo on pg. 86)

While chilling out at a Sports Bar in Amsterdam, Holland on a Saturday evening in 2008, who do I see on the TV, but the 1978 Dallas Cowboys playing the Washington Redskins. I'm sure this was an NFL classics production, yet I didn't expect to see this in Europe. I was sure that nobody would believe me, so I pulled out my iPhone and snapped photos.

Getting an opportunity to design and produce hooded jackets for the whole Dallas Cowboys Super Bowl team was such a thrill, because it meant very high visibility and exposure.

Four days before the Cowboys boarded a flight to Miami, to play the Pittsburg Steelers for Super Bowl X, I took a first sample of a hooded Jacket to my friend Harvey Martin (Super Bowl XII MVP), to see if he could help me get permission to sell them to the public.

In celebration of our nations 200th birthday, the 1976 prototype had a special bicentennial stars and stripes design. The design blended with the Cowboys Star, and a white Super Bowl X silk screened on slate blue (Cowboys color) poly-cotton taffeta material, front and back, with Dallas Cowboys Super Bowl X embroidered in bold white satin script on the front pocket.

Harvey called me later that day and said he had good, and bad news; the bad news first, the NFL office in New York would have to look at the design to determine if the NFL copyrights were infringed upon, which could take several weeks; and the good news is that he had orders from the whole team for the jackets. He said, "come and get the list of names and sizes". I was so thrilled, and so inexperienced that I didn't bother to ask Harvey about the payment.

Making 100 Jackets in three days - because many players ordered two and three jackets for their family members - with silk screened designs on the front and back, and embroidered names on each one, was a big challenge even for a company much larger than mine. This required teamwork, and wow did we have it.

My team, from the piece goods supplier Haber Fabrics in Irving, TX, to the cutter, Hubert Johnson and Company, to the silk screeners/embroiderers, and my Aunt Margaret, Aunt Connie, and their crews; we were all in it, to win it, for our team. We were Super Bowl bound. The Cowboys, that is.

We all felt connected to the team, through the order. We all worked fervently to deliver those jackets, and not let our team down, knowing that they would do their part on the field, and bring us back the Super Bowl trophy we deserved.

I was hailed as hustler extraordinaire by all my business associates for pulling off this feat. None of them ever appeared to doubt that we would deliver in three days. During this time, I needed extra cash to make things happen faster, and get the quickest turnaround from my team. I turned to someone that I knew believed in me and trusted me very much; my former basketball coach from Zumwalt Jr. High School, Coach Wiley.

He gladly delivered the money and cheered me on. My enthusiasm and confidence, as leader of the production, certainly helped our team's effort. To motivate our crew, I asked All-Pro Wide Receiver Drew Pearson, and Tight End Billy Joe DuPree to stop by and visit the production shops. They did and it was a blast for the crews.

When we examined the orders by name and sizes, my Aunt Margaret called to my attention that we did not have an order from Tom Landry, the Head Coach, or Quarterback Roger Staubach.

She said, "we have to make one for them too. Make them extra-large". I never argued with her, she was wise, she loved me, and I knew it. She always had my best interest at heart. So, I put their names on the list to be monogrammed, even though they didn't order, and didn't pay.

Three days later, we delivered right in the nick of time. We had worked around the clock. The players were gathering to board the flight to Miami, boarding at the old Braniff Airlines terminal, on Lemmon Ave. Love Field Airport. The silkscreen and embroidery, which was the final part of the production, came very close to our deadline of getting the jackets on the plane with the team.

I had just picked up the jackets from the embroidery shop, where we had each player's name put on. We parked as close as possible to the fence that separated the players from the fans, and carried the jackets to the fence, calling out the players names, as I tossed the jackets over the fence, just before they boarded the plane. Whew!! Close call, but we did it!!!

Anyone who thinks that my confidence was not shaken, and that I was never nervous about this whole ordeal, with all the Super Star athletes and business associates, would be sadly mistaken. There were times at the beginning of this venture, when I was so nervous my voice would break, and I could hardly get the words to come out.

I stopped to think about the gravity of who, and what I was dealing with, and at 23 years old, it almost overwhelmed me. I pulled myself together, and regained some self confidence about who I am, and what I deserved for my hard work, and moved forward with the project."

The fact that I was so excited, I took this order without securing terms of payment for the sale, taught me a painful and expensive lesson. This turned out to be a bad mistake that would take most of the Cowboys off season, spring, and summer to collect payments from the players. The transaction debacle damaged relationships with some of my contractors, because it took me so long to pay them. The realities of an under-financed manufacturing operation can have abrupt and severe consequences.

The Cowboys lost Super Bowl X to the Steelers. My friend Harvey and several of the other Pro Bowl players did not even return to Dallas right after the Super Bowl, mostly because the Pro Bowl in Hawaii was scheduled for the following week. Quite a few of the players traveled directly to Hawaii immediately after leaving Miami.

When Harvey did return, he was in a real foul mood, nursing several nagging injuries from an extremely long grueling season including the playoffs, and with the agony of barely loosing the Super Bowl, he had a right to be in a bad mood. I didn't blame him, but I needed to get paid for the jackets that we made and delivered. I went to Too Tall, and he helped me get in touch with most of his teammates over the spring and summer to collect.

Chapter IX

Custom Sportswear for the Dallas Cowboy Players

For anyone who doubts the phenomenal international influence the Cowboys had in the 70s, you only have to look at the photo of an 18 month old baby who happened to be the Prince of Cambridge, and heir to the throne of Britain, Prince William as a toddler wearing a Cowboy jersey in 1983. Now that's juice.

Tony Dorsett, Too Tall Jones, Robert Newhouse, and Thomas "Hollywood" Henderson were just a few of the players that we custom outfitted in Grand Stand (my label) Jumpsuits, and two piece denim suits. Which were the most challenging and why? I can still remember Too Tall's 24" thighs, and 42" inseam, and Robert Newhouse's 28" thighs and 32" waist, what a challenge to make custom jeans for him, but we did it. Even though there were many more like Drew Pearson, Harvey Martin, Billy Joe Dupree, Butch Johnson, Tony Hill, Bennie Barnes, and Mel Renfro, who bought custom made apparel from me, there was no challenge bigger than correctly fitting the anatomy of the first group.

On a typical day during the seasons of 1975 through 1978 I was a regular at the Dallas Cowboys locker room. One evening after practice, Tex Schramm, the General Manager came through the front door of the locker room, when Harvey, Too Tall, Tight End Jean Fugett (brother of the legendary Wall Street tycoon Reginald F. Lewis), my assistant and myself both dressed in suits, were standing on the steps to the front door, wearing my promotional Grand Stand Football Jerseys.

Left to right; Harvey Martin, James Jefferson, Ed "Too Tall" Jones

We were getting ready to take the promotional photos, ***presented herein.*** Tex Schramm said "hey Harvey, are you making your own jerseys now?", We all just laughed with Tex a little, and he was gone in seconds. Tex Schramm was the undisputed most powerful General Manager in the NFL at the time, yet he didn't push his weight around. He could have ego tripped, pressed the issue, and told me to leave since I had no official business with the team. So secure with himself was Tex Schramm that he respected his players enough to give them their space. Even though I never got a chance to know him, I had immense respect for the way he handled that situation. Harvey believed in me and often did things to help my business.

I would sometimes show my newest designs from the trunk of my car, when players were leaving practice. When the players saw something they liked, I would go inside the locker room, or go to the players home, and take measurements for making the custom garments.

I knew I was in the presence of greatness on every encounter with this group, because I always watched each player very astutely during their games. However, we may have all taken their greatness for granted, just a little bit. The late Harvey Martin who died of pancreatic cancer December 24, 2001, was not only a Super Bowl MVP for the Cowboys, he was a good friend of mine since Zumwalt Junior High School.

Harvey was the primary reason I got an opportunity to produce clothing for the team, and subsequently make custom garments for Harvey and his many teammates. Harvey was one of the quickest Defensive Ends to ever play the game. He still holds the NFL record for quarterback sacks in a single season, although the NFL did not officially count quarterback sacks until 1982, the Cowboys credited Harvey with 23 sacks in 1977-78, the same year he was Super Bowl XII MVP. To this day no NFL defensive player besides Harvey has ever had more than 22.5 quarterback sacks in one season.

Harvey Martin had several nicknames but to most people who knew him through his youth into adulthood, he was just Harvey. Virtually everyone who knew him well, loved, and respected him. Mostly because he was about the most happy-go-lucky ordinary guy you ever met. Harvey was big, but never the biggest guy on our school campus.

Ultimately what we all came to know about Harvey was that he was blessed with a very big heart, that would show loyalty, honesty, and concern that covered his family and friends back. That same big heart propelled him to success against overwhelming odds in the NFL.

Harveys' passion for life, and will to win was amazing, and second to no one that I know. He literally willed himself starting at zero to the pinnacle in the world of Pro Football all in a matter of seven years. He did not play sports at all, until he was a junior in high school. Fortunately, Harvey had a lot of support from very successful peers, and coaches which helped him attain the aggression, and technique he needed to be successful. He frequently credited teammates and coaches from High School like Burnis McFarland, and Richard Harris, and Coach Norman Jett, to former College teammate Dwight White, formerly of the Pittsburg Steelers, and Mean Joe Greene, to Cowboy Hall Of Fame teammate Rayfield Wright, and others.

Even with all the support he received from coaches and peers, he had to work harder than most naturally talented athletes who were gifted with exceptional athleticism.

He was a very extroverted man with a giant personality. He owned restaurants, and night clubs, hosted his own radio program, and was a Sports Reporter for the Local CBS affiliate in his off season. Harvey was a quintessential South Side athlete from the 60's and 70's which is to say that he understood fashion and appreciated it. One look at the photo I took of him two weeks before Super Bowl XII in which he won the MVP award, and you will see what I mean; a white cashmere scarf accents a $25,000. custom-made Silver Fox, fur coat.

Harvey Martin, January 1978

An ice storm was forecasted for that night, so the fur coat was right on time. About 1:00am I suggested we go outside so I could take a picture of him in that awesome fur coat. The sunglasses were a Neiman Marcus product, and we both bought the same model.

The Cowboys had the number one Defense and Offense in the NFL at the time and were rich with top caliber players in every position on the field.

The clincher for me making sales to the Cowboys started three days before the team boarded a flight to Miami for SuperBowl X. The whole team, with only a few exceptions ordered for themselves and family members. When I delivered those roughly 100 jackets in just three days, as they were boarding the team airplane at the Braniff terminal Love Field airport, they were convinced. From that point on, the players knew that I would deliver good quality, on time.

The Dallas Cowboys All-Pro wide receiver, Drew Pearson became a good customer and a friend. Drew was often called Mr. Clutch because of so many crucial catches when the game was on the line, and the Cowboys had to have the catch to win the game. Drews' legendary "Hail Mary" catch will forever be remembered in NFL history, and has helped him be named one of the top ten Dallas Cowboys to ever play. When Drew stopped by the engineering office that I worked for near downtown Dallas, to pick up a blue denim outfit that I designed for him, the ladies in the front office went wild. I alternated engineering jobs with my passion for fashion, because it was part of my survival kit. I would not have survived even back then without another optional stream of cash-flow.

Drew was supportive in a few ways and accepted my invitation to come out and meet my piece goods (fabric) supplier, who had been clamoring to meet both Drew, and Harvey. Mr. Robbins owned Haber Fabrics, the largest piece goods warehouse, and wholesale operation in the Dallas area, at the time. Mr. Robbins and his young faithful General Manager Richie were delighted to host Drew. Richie, and Mr. Robbins took us for a short tour of the massive warehouse.

After the tour the four of us went to Mr. Robbins office to chat. We laughed and talked about the Cowboys success on the football field for a while. Mr. Robbins told Drew how much he liked me, and he said, "Stan is a good designer who really knows what the people want". "You should back Stan with money to finance his business operation". I was utterly shocked, in a pleasant way of course.

I had no idea that Mr. Robbins was going to say such a thing. I did not know that he respected me or liked me the way he said. At twenty-two years old, I had a lot to learn about winning friends and influencing people. The Haber Fabrics General Manager Richie, who was a whiz-kid, probably in his late twenties or early thirties at the time, would occasionally pull me to the side and advise me on some complex decisions. Afterwards, I couldn't help but believe that Drew must have thought he had been set up, for this pitch to back my manufacturing operation. I observed and listened, joining in the conversation very little. Drew agreed with Mr. Robbins on my assets as a designer, but was very reserved, and non-committal, about financially backing my operation.

Mr. Robbins wasn't done, like the seasoned veteran that he was, he had a plan B. He asked Drew what he had planned for the off season. Drew replied that he would definitely be catching up on leisure time. Mr. Robbins then asked how often Drew got back home to visit family and friends in New Jersey. Drew replied that it wasn't often enough or something to that effect. This was the prelude to an offer by Mr. Robbins for Drew to do periodic meet and greet Public Relations when Mr. Robbins, and Richie flew to New York on business trips.

One day while driving through Downtown Dallas around lunchtime, I heard on the radio that Drew Pearson would be signing autographs at Bonds Men's Store on Main St. I had a little extra time on my hands so I thought I would go by the store and see Drew. I got there just a little early, and very few people had shown up, in fact there was only four or five people there with me. I knew that we were ten to fifteen minutes early, so I decided to look around the store a little while waiting for Drew to show up. After waiting for another twenty minutes or so, more Cowboy fans begin to show-up in the store, and there we were waiting for Drew to show up and sign autographs. While moving between merchandise racks in the store as I looked for shirts in my size, a fan came over and asked me for my autograph. I thought it was a joke, so I smiled and played along signing my name on her note pad. I kind of giggled and waited for the punch line.

She thanked me and walked away with no punch line. Before I could turn around and walk away, another fan asked for an autograph, then another. It began to sink in for me that these fans thought I was Drew.

I was flattered but confused because I did not see any resemblance between Drew Pearson and myself. The main thing Drew and I had in common was that we were both well dressed, young Black men in our early twenties. I thought wait til I tell Drew about this. We'll both get a good laugh out of this. After I signed one more autograph in my name, not Drews', - which the fans paid no attention to, until they walked away - I decided to get out of there before it got any crazier.

The next day I went to Drews locker after practice and told him what happened. Drew was not amused at all by this story. He said everybody knows Drew Stan. I couldn't stop myself from laughing because he was serious as a heart attack. I thought it was hilarious, and he felt offended at the notion that Cowboy fans would show up to get his autograph and mistake me for Mr. Clutch Drew Pearson.

He was really pissed off because I couldn't stop laughing. The more pissed off I saw him get, the funnier it was to me. Drew would not have showed up for the meeting with my fabric supplier or stopped by to visit my Aunts' sewing shop if he wasn't my friend. I asked him to make both of these visits as a personal favor that would support my new business venture.

However, there was no doubt in my mind, he wanted to knock me out. That's when I came to understand the ego of an NFL ALL-PRO wide receiver. It is truly a unique entity in the wide world of sports.

I was very fortunate to get to know so many world class athletes who were teammates of my friend Harvey. They were among the absolute best in the NFL, and no doubt the best in the world. Because they respected Harvey immensely and were his friends as well as teammates, I was warmly accepted. That didn't guarantee me anything. I found that out the hard way, and what happened a short time later emphasized this point.

Too Tall was not just tall, he is a bigger than life football legend. The first number one pick in the NFL, for the Dallas Cowboys in their entire history came in 1974 when Ed "Too Tall" Jones was the first player picked in the NFL draft. Being a fashion-conscious man myself I still remember the really sharp plaid suit and bowtie Too Tall wore at the 1974 NFL Draft. Too Tall was a former basketball, and baseball player, who's first love was boxing. He excelled at all four sports and was lured by professional organizations of all four sports prior to deciding on a career in the NFL.

At 6'-9" Too Tall was one of the hand full of players on the team who really needed a tailor, or someone to make custom fitted clothing for him. During those days ready to wear garments for a man who stood almost 7' were slim pickings, and very limited selections even in Big and Tall men's stores. Besides we were all in our early twenties and men's fashion in the

70s was about expressing yourself. His friendship with Harvey Martin, lead him to an ideal person who could handle the big task. Little Tim Jackson, a mutual friend and classmate of Harvey and myself in High School, and Jr. High, was an excellent choice.

Tim was a very good tailor. He was meticulous and detail oriented, and he knew the clothing business well, because he was the best dressed High School boy we had ever seen in the Dallas public schools. "Too Short" was the nickname that the 5'-5" Lil Tim choose for himself, after becoming Tailor for Too Tall. Tim had the 2SHORT vanity license plates on his extra-long 1973 Lincoln Continental Town Car. What a site. This makes me laugh every time I see it in my memory.

When it was clear to me that most of the team didn't come back to Dallas directly from Super Bowl X, and instead went to the NFL Pro-Bowl held a week later in Hawaii, I knew I was in trouble. I went to Too Tall for help getting in touch with his teammates so I could collect for the jackets I delivered as they boarded the jet to SuperBowl X. Too Tall made it his business to see that I got paid.

People who didn't follow the stats, or the play by play very well may have thought Hollywood Henderson was mostly hype because he was surrounded by All-Pro teammates. However, his 4.7 seconds of running the forty-yard dash, was the absolute fastest of any linebacker in the NFL at that time. Not only was he fast, he made tackles with authority.

For anybody who doubts this, the proof clearly shows itself in the 1978 YouTube video of Thomas Henderson doing what most people thought was impossible; taking down Earl Campbell solo. Earl Campbell made a living running over solo tackles and is clearly established as being in the top 3 power running backs of all-time in NFL history. So good was Hollywood Henderson, that Lawrence Taylor, who many football fans consider the best Linebacker to ever play the game, said that he was so inspired by Thomas Henderson that he chose to wear his number 56.

Because I was twenty-two to twenty-five years old during this timeframe, and the majority of my Cowboy clients were within two years of my age, you might wonder about the many wild parties that the Cowboys have long been remembered for.

In the 1960s and 70s the Cowboys were notorious for being brash, bold, and wild, and for partying like rock stars. The teams of 1975 through 1980s certainly held up their part of this legacy. Things really did start to get a little wild when Thomas" Hollywood" Henderson came to the Cowboys.

Someone must have told Thomas Henderson he could sing, because he used to sing his favorite song in the locker room all the time. "Sara Smile" by Hall and Oats was what you could hear him sing after practice. Thomas Henderson and Too Tall Jones shared a house in Garland during the times that I made custom sportswear for them, and he would often sign "Sara Smile" at home.

We produced probably the most impeccable custom One-Suit that we ever made for Hollywood Henderson, in my opinion. It was the same style as what is pictured below yet the fabric was a plush cordless corduroy, with a cinnamon hounds' tooth pattern, very much like the salt and pepper pattern, but brown and beige, instead of black and white, pictured below. It was very unique. (continued on next page)

Men's Sportswear Model wearing Grand Stand "One-Suit" - October 1976. First purchased by Dallas Cowboys Legendary Linebacker, Thomas "Hollywood" Henderson.

The old stories about the Cowboys of the 60s when Quarterback Don Meredith was the focus of a Motion Picture titled "North Dallas Forty", got a real challenge from this group from the late seventies.

One night my lady, and I were at a K104 Radio station party, in the ballroom of the Marriott Market Center. We were guest of Radio Personality Sherry Jones. There were 8 to 10 people (mostly couples) setting at a large table with us which included a high-profile beauty from Amsterdam, Holland; Holley Lemons (***The name has been changed to protect her innocence)***, and her boyfriend. Holley was God's gift to men, by her own estimation, and the close friend to a lady that I had dated previously. Holley and my former girlfriend were together when we first met at the night club called "Place Across The Street" owned and operated by my homie Cecil Partee.

My former girlfriend told me that when we met at the club that night Holley told her "you can have him". Get the picture about Holley? When Holley realized that Thomas "Hollywood" Henderson was at the radio station's party, she went to him, they talked and in minutes they were both out of there.

She left her boyfriend at the party to drown in embarrassment, because almost everyone at the party knew exactly what happened to his gorgeous girlfriend. He stayed for two hours or so, trying not to look so humiliated. We all looked at him out of the corners of our eyes and thought "wow, bad night huh?"

Holley and Thomas Henderson didn't come back to the party that night. I couldn't wait to see him in the Cowboys locker room the next day so I could ask him all about it. Hollywood was eager to talk about the event.

As soon as I saw him, I asked and he responded, "Man that b---- kept on purring in my ear like a big pussy cat, then as soon as we finished up in bed, she ask for the keys to my new Benz (Mercedes-Benz)." This was really funny to me, and very predictable because as I told him, I dated her girl friend, and she had her own signature sound effects.

However, Holleys' sound effects were awesome, and I knew it, because two weeks before the radio station's party, she purred in my ear as we slow danced at "The Place Across the Street" (Night Club). This was the hottest club in town at the time. It is where I saw Chaka Khan after one of her concerts, partying with her date - Thomas Hollywood Henderson.

At the age of twenty-three, I had no frame of reference for the thrill, and turn on this super sexy lady, with the heavy Dutch accent was giving me, on the dance floor, as we slow-danced to "The Love Ballad" by LTD. As I held her firm in my arms while we danced, her curvaceous, and voluptuous body melted into my fingers on her hips, and then she put her tongue right in my ear, and bellowed out the most pelvic and sexy pussy cat purr that you could ever imagine.

Her body felt like jello (no bones) squishing through my grasp. The combination was tremendous. That feel of her body, and that deep slow pelvic pussy cat purr, which actually had more pussy in it than any 5'-7" 125lb pussy cat could ever produce, was transcendent. Hollywood seemed to be annoyed by the purring. I thought it was the best thing since sliced bread. I couldn't figure out whether he was more annoyed by

Holley purring in his ear, or her asking for the keys to his new Mercedes Benz right after they had sex. If Holley's purr was just something that rolled off her lips, it might be kind of funny, but this was no joke. That purr came from her whole body, it was bellowed out from her pelvis like a song.

This was all on another level for me. I have this theory that she had the skill of drawing a voice from her vagina through her vocal cords. To me that purr said "I am pussy, hear me, feel me, etc. etc." Since I had never experienced anything like this before or afterwards, I figured it must be a European thing. In July of 2008 I traveled to Amsterdam in search of this cultural phenomenon, to no avail.

Oh yeah Holley's friend whom I dated, had her own most unique deep pelvic moan when we made love. So unique, and such a turn on was this sound effect, that I couldn't wait to tell one of my home boys who I had not seen in weeks. As I described this phenomenal pelvic part song, part moaning sound to my friend, he listened intently, when I finished, he asked me "where did you say the girl lives again". I said the Village. (The Village was the largest apartment community in Dallas. It spanned about twenty blocks) Then I described the specific area. He said, "man I think I have some bad news for you". "There was this Jamaican guy who is one of my neighbors, he was here just a few days ago, and he described the same sound effects with who I believe is the same girl". Then I remembered, that was the weekend I spent in Houston. I was shocked, and she was history.

When Tony Dorsett AKA "The Aliquippa Flash" (from Aliquippa, PA) came to join the Cowboys in 1976, as the latest Heisman Trophy winner, and the top pick in the NFL draft, his entourage came with him. There was a half dozen of Dorsett's former teammates and friends living with him. I would go to his house on a few occasions to take measurements for custom designs. J-Harv was one of the housemates that I got to know. He was a real cool, fun loving guy, who was a lot like Dorsett in that regard.

A funny thing happened during a transaction when Dorsett was paying for an outfit that I designed for him. He gave me a check for the purchase, and I accidentally gave it back to him, because I was so nervous.

I was dressing the top running back in the NFL, the latest Heisman Trophy winner in my own Grand Stand label. He said, "Stan that check is good anywhere, why you giving it back to me." He seemed offended. He then said, "Stan I don't need your money." Yes, that was not just funny, it was embarrassing for me. As I got to know Dorsett better, I was invited to hang out with them and do some bar hopping at nightclubs. We would roll eight to ten cars deep when we arrived at the clubs, when you heard "The Hawk", - as Dorsett liked to be called by friends - , say "drinks on the house", you knew the par-tae was on. We partied like rock stars.

Chapter X
Downs and Walls Sporting Goods Store

In 1981, I became business Partners with two of the Dallas Cowboys. Rookie Defensive Backs Everson Walls, and Michael Downs were both natives of Dallas, and when Hall Of Fame running back Tony Dorsett could not decide on whether or not to accept the partnership deal I offered him. The two Homies did. Our many clients at the Sporting Goods Store included some of the elite Night Clubs in Dallas, and Ft. Worth, for promotional polo shirts, t-shirts, and jackets.

There were also many Restaurants and other Corporate Clients including UCCELL Corp. Pro-Line Corp. for Trophies, Plaques, Awards, and Certificates all sold through the Sporting Goods Store. Amateur Little League basketball, and baseball teams, amateur adult basketball, baseball, and soccer teams became good customers for my sales staff.

My two business partners were excelling on the football field, as Downs became a starter at safety before the first regular season game. Everson soon cracked the starting line-up at cornerback, after making several interceptions when given the opportunities to play.

Because of my previous experience at the Apparel Mart, I was able to act as a tour guide for my two young partners when we went to the Apparel Mart to buy merchandise for the store. During our visits there, it was clear for me to see that the boom times of the 60's and 70's at the Apparel Mart was over, and the gradual decline was in the works.

The wholesalers in the showrooms we visited were excited to meet Mike and Everson, yet they seemed to not really take them serious as businessmen, since they were 22-year-old Dallas Cowboy rookies. Our store was located in what I thought was a high traffic, strip shopping center, because there was a Target Store one half block behind us, and a K-Mart store one block on the adjacent corner. Not only that, the demographic study that I conducted showed that there were healthy middle-class income residential areas bordering the store to the west, and south. Despite the apparent potential, it all looked better on paper, and in the demographic study, than it proved to be in reality.

None of the retail stores, large or small in this area were able to survive the whims of the economy, and the change in buying patterns. Consequently, two years after we closed our doors because of continual negative cash-flows, the K-Mart store which was on the adjacent corner to our store, closed and was converted to a mini-mall. Shortly afterwards the Target store was closed, and the building converted to a Mini-mall which became one of the most notorious venues in Texas for black market merchandise; Big T Bazaar.

Chapter XI

The East Coast Connection

This chapter has the least to do with fashion or apparel making, yet without it, I doubt that this book would be possible. I would definitely not be the person that I am today without my east coast connection.

For the record my East Coast connection predates me by well over 160 years. You see I have ancestral roots in Baltimore, MD. My Great-Great Grandfather Samuel Beecham was a free man who lived in Baltimore around 1850. He was tricked into helping two strangers who were evil white men that captured him, took him to the south where slavery was legal, and sold him into the system.

This story has been well known in my maternal family for many years and may have tremendous influence on the most unusual feeling of DeJa Vu that I ever felt in life upon my first visit to Baltimore. I knew beyond any shadow of a doubt that I had seen the sites of Baltimore before, on my first visit. I never experienced such a strong feeling like that before in my life. Nor have I experienced a feeling so rare since that first visit to Baltimore.

Shortly after we closed the Downs and Walls Sporting Goods Store in 1983, I started a Contract Engineering job for Texas Instruments on the headquarters campus in Richardson, Texas. The nature of engineering contractor work is unstable to the 4th power, very vulnerable to corporate budget whims, and economic downturns. The field of engineering was not my first choice, but I have been blessed with it for a very long career.

I knew that I had creative skills in art, and fashion, but for whatever reason, I thought that creative talent had a nexus with writing, so I got this bright idea to write a book in 1984. I pondered this idea for a few months and decided it could work. I flew to Washington DC to talk with my cousin who is a Psychologist about this idea, and ironically my cousin is also a former high school dropout who later reconsidered his educational endeavors.

Guy Ruth from Yonkers, New York, married my first cousin Eunice Scurlark from Monahans, Texas. To this happy union two terrific young men were born and raised; Bobby and Allen (both now deceased). The whole family thought a great deal of Guy because of his academic achievement, and jovial personality.

Before I pursued this goal of writing a book, I wanted to find out what Guy thought of it. He listened to my ideas about the book and gave his take on it, which was very moderate, not at all enthusiastic. This was OK with me since he didn't think the idea was ridiculous. The bottom line was that I just believed Guy was not at all convinced that I had the courage and wherewithal to finish the task.

Even though I didn't quite know what I was getting into, and how much this book would challenge me, I was convinced that I could do it. I proceeded to pull together ideas from friends and associates by hosting a dinner for some of the top Coaches, and Pro Athletes in Dallas at a Luxury Hotel (The Grand Kepinski, now called the Intercontinental Hotel (in Addison, TX).

We talked for hours as I tried to pick their brains for nuggets that I believed would help sell my books. This dinner conference was surprisingly unproductive, and for that time, it overrated my value of synergism. However, it helped me focus on how much work I had to do, if this project was going to have any chance at all.

As I continued to work a full-time job and write on weekends, the book content developed. After being laid-off at Texas Instruments, (the first of four times, due to economic downturns) I decided to pursue a job as a Mechanical Designer in Washington DC. I had visited my cousins, and former High School friends there several times, and thought it would be a good place to live.

I was successful in my job search, so I relocated, and consequently finished my first book "The Reality Trip" in 1987 while living in Silver Springs, MD, a suburb of Washington DC. "Washington D.C. is a city of southern efficiency, and northern charm", that's what beloved President John F. Kennedy said. Washington DC is a richly cultured international city, with a great fashion sense. I felt right at home, although it was a very different atmosphere in many ways. There was a very familiar vibe about it for me because I had family and friends there. I visited my friend Robert

Andrews, several times before I moved there, and he was well connected in DC culture.

I was lucky to have a friend like Robert who knew exactly what was going on around town. We went to the coolest parties and cruised the Baltimore Inner Harbor on Sunday evenings. I took my three – Joy-Bringers children, Nicole almost 2, Kerwin 6, Marci 16 - paddle boating on the Baltimore Inner Harbor on a gorgeous sunny and mild Sunday evening. What a beautiful day!!

All the spectacular museums and monuments in DC gave my three children, and family plenty of options, and we visited all the museums and monuments we could find. My three children were all school age at the time, so the Smithsonian Children's Museum was a hit with my six-year-old son Kerwin. working on Capitol Hill at The Architect Of The Capitol, I was able to get my youngest daughter Nicole in to see the underground Vaults in the U.S. Capitol building during a Halloween night event for employees.

There were plenty New Yorkers in DC. I became friends with several natives of Harlem, The Bronx, Queens, Brooklyn, Bed-Stuy, and Long Island. Because New York City was only a short flight away, - less than one hour from DC -, we all made frequent trips there on the weekends. Our objective was to party and have a good time. Towards this end, I experienced one the most unique parties ever, as we went to a massive three level, multi-venue party on the USS Intrepid Aircraft Carrier, anchored in the Hudson River banks. This time frame in 1985-87 was a period that introduced me to NYC like never before.

I discovered lower Manhattan, SoHo, and 14th Street first, and then about two months later even deeper into Lower Manhattan, I discovered China Town, and Canal Street. That's when I discovered the black market on steroids. **More details of my Black-Market experiences are shared in Chapter XIII.**

One of my biggest joys in life is to have had the honor of leading a corporate board of eight luminaries for a Washington DC non-profit educational consulting organization. I co-founded the 501c3 organization, and personally recruited all eight people; four of which were Ph.Ds. Along with their stellar credentials, they were an absolute delight to work with. John X. Miller – the Olympics editor for USA Today at that time (1988) - was the first.

I was introduced to John by a mutual friend who happens to be the most prolific writer I know; Roland Lazenby, who has authored over sixty sports biography books. John became my faithful confidant, right hand man, and co-founder of the educational consulting operation. James F. Brown, the sports announcer for CBS NFL Today, who gave my first book a glowing endorsement, became an advisor.

Through networking with my good friend from Bed-Stuy (Brooklyn) Alan Watson, a top salesman with Xerox at the time, I was introduced to a top executive of the telecom giant MCI - Mel Forbes. After I delivered an impassioned presentation, Mel was all in. Shortly afterwards Dr. James C. Moone, a Georgetown University professor, and ordained minister became another advisor.

Again, my friend Alan Watson got the bright idea that I should go and talk to Dr. Vincent Reed, vice president of communications for the Washington Post. Dr. Reed was also former under-secretary of education in the Reagan administration, and the longest tenured superintendent in the Washington DC public schools' modern history.

Dr. Reed granted my request for a meeting at his office, and we began a friendship, mentorship, that has been extremely rewarding in my life. Dr. Reed became my closest, and most trusted advisor. Immediately after a radio interview with the number one rated Sunday morning talk show in Detroit Michigan, I received a call from a local physician who wanted a copy of my book, and to discuss some common ground. On the other end of the phone was non other than Dr. Cynthia Shelby-Lane, the dynamic force of nature, packaged in a stand-up comedian/emergency room physician hybrid persona. I mailed the book to her immediately, and we began to talk, and plan our collaboration. In a short time, she began co-presenting the workshops with me, and our production was enhanced tremendously.

Our volunteer group focused on character development, through the emphasis of Crime and Violence Prevention educational programs (workshops, and seminars) for inner-city high school students, and faculty. We also produced educational videos.

There were two more board members that I recruited through a high-profile conference held at Howard University. Meeting and actually having a personal conversation with Arthur Ashe, the Legendary Tennis Player, made the event a very high-profile event for me.

The conference organizer Dr. Lee McElroy, Athletic Director, Sacramento State University, and Liz Galloway-McQuiter, Head Coach Ladies Basketball Lamar University supplemented our board. It was a thrill to work with everyone in this stellar group.

My life experience has been enhanced exponentially as a result our collaborations. While there were times when we disagreed on issues, we consistently looked for reasons to work together, instead of looking for reasons not to. I will always treasure the memories of working with such a brilliant and high-spirited group.

Chapter XII

Passion for Fashion

Fashion is the silent statement of identity, an expression of relevance in the universe. It expresses our love of art, our love of freedom, our joy of being here right now, our aspirations for the future. It has always been important to me.

My earliest memories of fashion are seared forever in my memory banks; My dear Aunt Rosie Scurlark (my father's sister now deceased) was a beautiful and charming lady. Aunt Rosie would buy me the most terrific shirts for Christmas and birthdays at four or five years old. The shirts were extraordinary and very high quality. My Aunt worked as a domestic cook and maid to one of the many very successful Jewish Apparel merchants in Dallas.

At that time, I was missing my two front teeth, and I couldn't speak very clearly. She would ask me "who bought that shirt for you", time, and time again, just so she could hear me say Aunt Rosie, which would always come out, "Unnt Woosie", and she would laugh with so much joy, and love, over, and over again. Her joy and love helped me appreciate the art of fashion. Through her passion my Aunt Rosie gave me so much more than just shirts.

My dear Aunt Rosie was a hardworking single mother of four, when she bought these shirts for me. Her love and devotion to family, including her nephew will never be forgotten.

When my one and only sibling, Vivian got her first job as a teenager, she wanted to buy me a gift with part of her first check. Lucky me. Anything I wanted she said, and as you might guess I choose clothes. Even at eleven years old. She wasn't surprised at all that I told her the exact color, size and where she should buy the sweater.

Shopping for High Fashion apparel and accessories was a favorite pastime to me for decades. Kind of like a sport, I have a passion for fashion like many other people I know. My girlfriend in high school, was just like me in this regard. She was voted best dressed girl in our high school class. We got married shortly after high school and gave birth to a beautiful baby girl we called Marci.

We would occasionally meet other friends and go shopping at Neiman Marcus, Dreyfuss & Son, Colbert's, J. Riggins, and boutiques such as DeJa Vu, and The Gazebo. Through the Woodstock era of the late 60's and 70's there was a legendary and iconic retail store called "The Gazebo". It was beyond any shadow of a doubt the coolest place in the south to shop for clothes. With numerous rock star celebrity clients, such as Led Zeppelin, The Gazebo was in a class of its own. Charles Bolton, the owner and founder of The Gazebo knew me as a frequent customer on a first name basis for several years. When he found out that I was launching a line of

Mens High Fashion Sportswear, he was happy to help co-ordinate my first fashion show. We were such regular customers at the Gazebo that we became friends with several managers, and members of the sales staff.

Ed Long was one of the Gazebo managers, who became a good friend. Ed and his wife would come to my apartment for parties, and we would periodically go to parties, and rock concerts together. We caught the unforgettable super-concert of the seventies; The Rolling Stones, and Stevie Wonder together with Jim, and Kim who also worked at the Gazebo.

Jim was also the lead singer for a local rock band called the Flag. Jim was way cool, very fashion forward, and of course to work on the sales staff at the Gazebo, you would have to be pretty cool. My friend Jim was also a friend, and former Phoenix area school mate of Rock Star Alice Cooper, whom Jim called Vincent.

We planned to go to one of his concerts and party with Alice Cooper after the show. We never got around to that, and I'm not sure I regret missing out on partying with Alice Coopers' big ass pet snake. Jim and I were bonded through our passion for fashion.

In 1975 when I launched my line of men's sportswear, the time came for my first fashion show. The fashion show production was a tremendous amount of work, designing, coordinating, and rehearsing. My team of models, student apprentices, and industry professionals, pattern makers and graders, all collaborated effectively, and we presented a really good show. Our audience at a brand-new night club, which was owned by channel 4 News Anchor-man Jay Ruffin, was not a sellout crowd but about 80% full yet very enthusiastic.

Chapter XIII

Fashion Detour into the Black Market

(The names have been changed to protect the innocent)

My passion for fashion would take me shopping in Washington DC, Georgetown, and Downtown; Philadelphia South Street, and Downtown; Baltimore, the Inner-Harbor and Downtown; New York City, all over midtown Macy's, Barney's. Bloomies, Saks, Bergdorf, Greenwich Village, Lower Manhattan, East Broadway (Century 21), SoHo, and Chinatown/Canal Street. As anyone who has shopped New York City knows, there's no place on earth like shopping in NYC.

It was one of these many shopping escapades in 1986 that I discovered well-made Swiss replica watches that looked extraordinarily authentic. I bought a few for myself, and my lady. Soon friends and relatives would comment on how good the watches looked. They of course would want to know how much the watches cost, and a little about the quality and performance. Next, they would very often ask me a question that I would hear over, and over for more than twenty years. They would ask me to get one for them, the next time I go back to New York.

My oldest daughter Marci is a hairstylist in a Washington DC suburb. Her specialty is weaves and extensions. Marci (my daughter) gained a level of success nationally as a Platform Artist with Bronner Brothers Hair Care products, and as a highly acclaimed trainer in her field.

When she got the great idea to start importing her own signature label of high grade remy cuticle human hair from India, and China for nationwide sales, she asked me to join her team as a partner and sales manager.

I thought it was a great opportunity, and I accepted her offer. As sales manager I began to call on upscale hair salons all over the Dallas Metroplex, as well as many other salons nationwide via the internet. My sales visits to hair salons all over the region brought me in contact with a variety of people who sold designer replica merchandise.

In as much as there are replica, and Black-Market merchandise such as sunglasses, jewelry, and purses in every major city in the United States, the fact exists that millions of people crossing all racial, religious, and socio-economic categories have bought black market merchandise. I use the terms replica, and black-market merchandise, because not all black-market merchandise, is replicas, or counterfeit. I know for a fact that there are many genuine items on the black market. This is a fact that many officials would rather not acknowledge or discuss. Moreover, one of the biggest mysteries in the fashion merchandising world for at least the last twenty years, is how much authentic basic raw materials go into the construction of what is considered counterfeits. Many celebrities, and otherwise wealthy people, and in some cases millionaires, choose to purchase black market merchandise for different reasons.

Often their purchases are made on the rationale that they are not concerned about durability, or longevity of a higher priced original. Like many American shoppers they are frequent shoppers, and have a large variety of designer originals, many of which never wear out physically, yet loose fashion freshness and appeal over time. One more thing about the originals, they cost a lot, $1,500 to $5,000. This underscores the motive for some millionaires and other wealthy people to buy replicas.

Quite often the replicas are so well made that it is not at all easy to determine that they are de facto counterfeits. In some cases, especially with trendier, fadish designs that are likely to be dated, and maybe even out of style in months as opposed to years, the replica offers options to make your choice. When its time to say goodbye after a few uses, in some cases a month or two, the frequent shopper doesn't feel so bad about parting with the $100. - $300. replica in comparison to the $1,500. to $5,000. genuine article.

As one of my very wealthy associates put it, "when I pay a lot of money for my merchandise, I feel really bad when it's time for me to get rid of it". In her case that could happen very shortly after purchase, because she is a de facto serial shopper, who frequently shops at Neiman-Marcus, Nordstrom's, Saks, and several boutiques at least three days a week.

Her attire is always flawlessly coordinated from head to toe, and even the best trained counterfeit spotter would be perplexed to point out what is, and what's not a replica in her vast wardrobe, filled with virtually everything imaginable, including real $5,000. Chanel purses, and the real $25,000 Rolex watches. Several replica products such as watches and purses which are sold in the black market, out number their retail originals in the marketplace.

In the early 2000's there was a surge in the supply of designer replica purses, shoes, watches and jewelry. There is a long list of evidence to indicate, that China spawned the surge of counterfeits worldwide, after gaining an economic boom from the surge of out-sourced production of American designer apparel, and accessories.

Because the U.S. spends more than three times as much as our closest rival nation on apparel, we essentially drive the world market for all has a much greater chance of being a successful product. Our 330million plus population, and mega purchasing power is very important to China, and all of the other Asian manufacturing countries. Plain and simple, it means business for them. It means jobs for their fragile economies, and a piece of the American dream that they have heard so much about in the past.

There were many outlets for distribution, with ladies in up-scale salons, to a long line of those who volunteer to have purse parties for a commission. When demand was high in the early 2000's, hustlers who had previously sold crack on the streets, would post up on a street corner in a heavily traveled intersection, and sale replica purses all day. These hustlers would gross more than $3,000. per day on the weekend with no trouble from the police.

There is one former drug dealer that I will never forget. He called himself Lil Vic. I never knew his complete real name. This was common for people who made a living in the black market. Some degree of anonymity was virtually always an objective.

There was no need for anyone to know the last names, because all transactions were cash and carry anyway. Checks for purchases were extremely rare, and even when checks were used, the payee would just fill in, the pay to, blank spot, to maintain a certain level of anonymity.

While driving down a busy street in my old neighborhood, I saw this little store that advertised all sorts of designer replica merchandise. I decided to stop and inquire, so I went in, and ask to speak to the owner. Lil Vic answered the inquiry and appeared a little paranoid, as he hesitantly introduced himself.

We talked for a while, and I told him that I had been a frequent shopper in New Yorks China Town. I showed him a few items that I bought in New York, and he began to drop his defensive behavior a little. I looked around his store and found a few really nice pieces.

After talking with him for months when I came in to buy merchandise, Lil Vic told me that he was once shot in the head and left for dead, when he used to sell crack cocaine. He showed me a very visible shotgun blast scar in the back of his head. The shot miraculously grazed his skull, instead of penetrating it.

He said it was a robbery by a rival who wanted him out of the business. He told me that his life changed a great deal after that miraculous survival.

He said he figured God saved him for a reason. Lil Vic's success didn't come easy, he was a bona fide hustler, who stayed after it, long hours, every day.

He was aggressive with expansion plans for other stores, and other businesses. Lil Vic was good with numbers, which I'm sure the crack business gave him a lot of practice at this skill. After law enforcement raided and confiscated all of the merchandise in Lil Vics store several times, he was out of business. It's not illegal to buy counterfeit merchandise but it is to sell it.

Ruth Rosenfeld was the self-proclaimed Grand Dame of black-market purses, and jewelry. She traveled from coast to coast selling designer replica purses, jewelry, and sunglasses. Ruth was a sophisticated, extroverted, and charming lady who had impeccable taste. She was always very well dressed, and because she was a seasoned veteran, you could see a bit of the 70's and 80's vintage haute couture in her style. She claimed to be the first person in Dallas to sale designer replica purses over thirty years ago, before she moved to LA. Ruth would rent two adjacent rooms at very nice garden hotels, in upscale communities to conduct business. Both rooms would be full of merchandise, flown in from New York, Las Vegas, and Los Angeles.

Ruth who lived in Los Angeles would book two to three days at hotels in major cities all across the country, as she periodically took her show on the road, circulating flyers at elite hair salons in each city on her tour to promote the showing dates. Because of her refined sense of style, and sophistication, Ruth was able to present her expertise about the quality details of her replica jewelry, and purses, and would often pass on this knowledge to customers.   Ruth's charm and sophistication won the confidence of her many happy customers from coast to coast, who benefitted from her knowledge.

There were many distributors of black-market purses, shoes and jewelry, but few more successful than one young man from Philadelphia, PA, who we called Sly. He was not much of a physical presence at 5'-7" about 150lbs. and shabbily dressed, with hardly ever a smile.

Unlike many hustlers whom I met through the salons, Sly had a small storefront, and an obvious plan to make a lot of money from his enterprise. When I first met Sly, he would have one or two of his friends watch the store front when he had to venture out to meet customers.

The friends who helped Sly watch the store, were either not very reliable, or not compensated for what they believed their time was worth, because they were not working with him long at all. Sales were always sluggish during the summer months, and when I met him that accounted for most of the suppressed business activity at Slys' store.

What Sly did have going for himself though, was an apparent vision, a small inexpensive storefront, a very strong work ethic, and really good New York connections, that would deliver large quantities of merchandise on a consistent basis. Sly was an unlikely success because his sales volume was not sufficient to cover his overhead. He was having a real hard time making ends meet.

When times were bad during the summer season, I vividly remember Sly telling me about a job he was pursuing. This job only paid $9. An hour, but he was desperate, and he needed the money for survival. I encouraged him to go for it, because the first order of business was keeping your head above water - survival. It doesn't matter how, just survive, by any, and all means necessary, then build on making things better as opportunities develop. He seemed to understand and told me he appreciated my advice.

Until he got his mother (Lizzie) involved with his operation, sales did not climb noticeably. Sly's Mom was a piece of work, a real hard-core hustler by nature. She was a single, mother of nine, who had a very distinct Bronx accent, cussed like a sailor, and had a fast city slick joke, and sales pitch for everyone she met.

Lizzie might have missed her calling as a gourmet chef, or a very good Stand –Up Comedian. Like many young mothers who were still growing-up with her children, after several encounters I never heard one of her children call her moma, or mother, instead they referred to her as Lizzie. Sly was her oldest child, and it was easy to see that they confided in each other immensely. Looking at their come up in retrospect, their contrasting personalities seem to complement each other.

Sly was reserved, serious, introverted, and rarely laughed, while Lizzie was vociferous, bubbly, almost always joking and laughing. Because both had a strong work ethic, they became a force to be reckoned with. There would be other family members like cousins, and a few siblings periodically working in the store as business began to grow, but the only constants in the success of their business venture was Sly, and Lizzie.

In no more than twenty-four months from the time that I met Sly, and shortly afterwards advised him to take that job for $9. an hour, he and his mother had built their sales to $10,000. a day (over $3million a year).

There is no exaggeration about the numbers, it was clear to see when 40 to 50 customers waited at the door for the store to open virtually every day of the week. Many of the customers were wholesalers who regularly spent $1,000. to $2,000. each. The law enforcement officers grew very suspicious of all the activity, and in a short time frame the law enforcement raided Sly's store and confiscated all of the merchandise in it. He and his family were out of business.

The consequences of being caught selling counterfeit merchandise, sometimes outweighs the profit motive. New laws have been created recently, that make the risk of being caught a much bigger deal than it was in 2003 or 2004. Local police forces now team with other law enforcement agencies, like the U.S. Marshalls, and the U.S. Customs and Border Patrol, because counterfeit merchandise is virtually always brought into the USA illegally. The New York Times reported on January 29, 2008, that a court agreement recently won by Louis Vuitton Matellier should go some way toward enforcing counterfeiting laws. In the agreement, certain Canal St. landlords will be required to post signs informing customers that vendors are not authorized Louis Vuitton dealers. Additionally, Vuitton and the landlords will be splitting the costs of an investigator who will have free access to inspect their properties at any time.

Canal Street customers looking for the best deals have been presented many clandestine adventures, by vendors trying to stay on the down low. Fake doors that double as display walls, and secret stairways to basement showrooms, have been topped by mobile showrooms.

In late 2009, thru early 2010 Cargo Vans with custom built shelving were stocked to the brim with designer replica purses, wallets, and belts, with just enough room for two people to fit in the back, and shop. These vans would park a half block off Canal Street and solicit customers. The drivers would always demand that you get in the van to shop, as opposed to just standing outside the van and looking in.

This new mobile shopping for black market goods proved to be a very unfortunate experience for two shoppers, who were inside the back of a van shopping, when the police came calling. The driver who was only thinking of evading the police, did not let them out. Consequently, the customers were detained for several hours after the van was stopped by police. There were seven vans filled with counterfeit purses busted that same day in China Town. All of the merchandise was confiscated, along with the vans, and the drivers arrested, according to police reports.

The increased pressure by law enforcement to curtail, or eliminate black market, and counterfeit merchandise has dramatically reduced the quantities of counterfeits available. With pressure being applied at virtually all levels of the chain, from factories in China, and other Asian countries, which are now scrutinized by private investigators, to U.S. Customs seizures of shipping companies' freight and cargo.

A crippling blow is being dealt to counterfeit designer merchandise worldwide. On our streets in the U.S. you can still find retailers who don't mind taking the risk of selling designer replicas, or counterfeits. However, in light of a sustained effort by law enforcement agencies, it is unlikely that the numbers will ever rival the number of retailers, and sales agents that existed during the peak times of 2002-2007.

Will designer replica or Black-Market merchandise cease to be sold because of the crackdown?

Unprecedented pressures are being leveled on the makers, and distributors of counterfeit, and Black-Market merchandise, from the factories throughout China, to the stores on Canal Street, and China Town, New York City, and all across the country.

Cyber stores on the internet are a much more menacing source for Designer Labels, evidenced by the fact that when you google replica watches, you get results for 8.6 million web sites, replica purses you get 5.5 million websites.

While shopping China Town I found many so-called replicas that were not copies at all in my opinion since the China town version was a different color, and in many cases a different material than the original. The fact that the designs were essentially the same, as a famous designer, caused these purses to fall into the category of replica or counterfeit.

Just as Victor Costa and other successful designers in the industry built their success on copies or inspirations from ideas which were not necessarily their own, so to must young designers have the freedom to reinterpret concepts that push the envelope, and offer consumers more choices of materials, colors and sizes.

The distinction of intellectual infringement, such as copying some one's logo, trademark, signature etc., is counterfeiting, and is the fine line that should not ever be crossed.

Fashion company Louis Vuitton reportedly spends $18.1 million each year in its anti-counterfeiting operations. In 2007, it had forty lawyers on staff and contracted 250 outside private investigators to assist in guarding its brand from counterfeits.

In 2007, luxury brand Louis Vuitton conducted over 7,600 anti counterfeiting raids and shut down more than 750 websites selling counterfeit Louis Vuitton products.

The lack of economic opportunities in the culture at large always stimulates black market activity, in some form or fashion. There is still a veracious demand for counterfeit and black-market merchandise, which is likely to rise with economic recovery. Because it is virtually impossible to police every factory in Asia twenty-four hours a day, or police all retail stores, or sales agents in America 24 hours a day, black markets find a way to adapt and survive against the odds.

As surely as people all over the world crave survival, the economics of black market and counterfeit merchandise dictate that they will exist in a diminished role for many years to come.

There are plenty of pontificating people who look down their nose at others who buy Black Market fashion merchandise, and others who say they are allergic to counterfeits. However reliable market analyst report that replicas outsell the original retail merchandise in many cases, so there have been a lot of people buying replicas. <u>*It is illegal to sell replica or counterfeit merchandise in the USA, but not to buy.*</u> In France it is illegal to even own replicas.

The issue of morality is complex when it applies to the law. For example, many laws are repealed year after year especially those that are considered victimless, such as marihuana, and alcoholic beverages. History has revealed numerous laws that were once illegal, and then changed to legal.

Lawyers who are sworn to defend clients that are conspicuously guilty of really heinous crimes such as rape, or murder sharpens the morality dilemma. Our legal system is a very complex one, which is abundant with dilemmas of morality. Our Criminal Justice system incarcerates more people per capita than any country in the world. The U.S.A. has more innocent incarcerations due to wrongful convictions than any country in the world.

Thanks to The Innocence Project we now have more criminal exonerations over the last decade, than any country in the world. Our laws, and our criminal justice system is a work in progress and is finally making some long overdue changes for the better. However, when we consider the fact that Judges, often make grossly erroneous and unjust decisions such as the Montana Judge who sentenced a 54-year-old man convicted of raping a 14-year-old girl to 30 days in jail.

The Judge crudely stated that the 14-year-old girl was mature beyond her chronological age, as though this somehow justified her being raped. There are cases far too numerous to mention - because it could fill this book - where Prosecutors, and Judges withheld, and/or suppressed evidence that could have cleared defendants.

This is where we start to see the very strong evidence that there is something wrong with our criminal justice system. I could point to literally hundreds of other examples where the evidence is blatantly and conspicuously unjust, but I think you get the picture. Although I find the exploitation of copying a designer's signature logo deplorable, I believe this practice will decline, as consumers become more knowledgeable about trademarks.

Consumers are feeling more and more like they are being taken advantage of when they pay large sums of money for merchandise that carry big trademarks, or logos. I often hear people say they feel like the designer is getting free advertisements, and they are paying for it. There is another segment of consumers that embrace the trademarks, and logos wholeheartedly because of the appearance of prestige.

The Hip-Hop culture which has enjoyed a significant influence on mainstream society for more than thirty years, fuels much of the demand for designer labels.

Top Hip-Hop artist like Jay-Z, Ludacris, LL Cool-J, and Kanye West, just to name a few, have made songs featuring lyrics about ladies' handbags by Louis Vuitton, Fendi, and Gucci. The vast majority of their fans cannot afford the real designer bags. Even for the small percentage of ladies who can afford the real bags, almost half of them are more inclined to buy a high-quality replica if it's available and keep the other 85% of the money they would pay in the stores.

Below is what a mammoth challenge confronts law enforcements agencies worldwide. This is the big picture, and the very reason that I believe, some forms of black-market activity in replica/counterfeit fashion products will continue.

Havoscope Ratings of Black Market Activities

1. Counterfeit Drugs$200 Billion
2. Prostitution$187.17 Billion
3. Counterfeit Electronics$169 Billion
4. Marijuana$141.80 Billion
5. Illegal Gambling$140 Billion
6. Cocaine$85 Billion
7. Prescription Drugs $72.5 Billion
8. Heroin$68 Billion
9. Software Piracy$63 Billion
10. Oil Theft$53.64 Billion
11. Illegal Tobacco$50 Billion
12. Counterfeit Foods$49 Billion
13. Counterfeit Auto Parts$45 Billion
14. Counterfeit Toys$34 Billion
15. Human Trafficking$32 Billion
16. Illegal Logging$30 Billion
17. Methamphetamine$28.25 Billion
18. Illegal Fishing$23.5 Billion
19. Human Smuggling$20 Billion
20. Wildlife Trafficking$19 Billion
21. Ecstasy$16.07 Billion
22. Music Piracy$12.5 Billion
23. Counterfeit Shoes$12 Billion
24. Counterfeit Clothing$12 Billion
25. Waste Dumping$11 Billion
26. Art Theft$10 Billion
27. Cable Piracy$8.5 Billion
28. Video Game Piracy$8.1 Billion
29. Counterfeit Sporting Goods$6.5 Billion
30. Counterfeit Pesticides$5.8 Billion
31. Bootlegging$4.3 Billion
32. Mobile Entertainment Piracy$3.4 Billion
33. Counterfeit Cosmetics$3.0 Billion
34. Movie Piracy$2.5 Billion
35. Metals and Minerals Smuggling$2.3 Billion
36. Counterfeit Aircraft Parts$2 Billion

37. Counterfeit Weapons$1.8 Billion
38. Kidnap and Ransom$1.5 Billion
39. International Adoptions$1.3 Billion
40. Fake Diplomas and Degrees$1 Billion
41. Arms Trafficking$1 Billion
42. Counterfeit Watches$1 Billion
43. Book Piracy$0.6 Billion ($600 Million)
44. Counterfeit Money$0.182 Billion ($182 Million)
45. Nuclear Smuggling$0.1 Billion ($100 Million)
46. Counterfeit IDs and Passports$0.1 Billion ($100 Million)
47. Organ Trafficking$0.075 Billion ($75 Million)
48. Counterfeit Purses$0.07 Billion ($70 Million)
49. Counterfeit Lighters$0.042 Billion ($42 Million)
50. Counterfeit Batteries$0.023 Billion ($23 Million)
51. Arms Trafficking$0.245 Billion ($245 Million)
52. Counterfeit Currency$0.182 Billion ($182 Million)
53. Nuclear Smuggling$0.1 Billion ($100 Million)
54. Counterfeit Cuban Cigars$0.1 Billion ($100 Million)
55. Organ Trafficking$0.075 Billion ($75 Million)
56. Counterfeit Purses$0.07 Billion ($70 Million)
57. Counterfeit Lighters$0.042 Billion ($42 Million)
58. Counterfeit Batteries$0.023 Billion ($23 Million)
59. Body Parts and Human Tissue$0.006 Billion ($6 Million)

The third sexiest Black Market Activity.

Although Black market purses, and watches rank 48, and 42, respectively on a list of the top black-market activities. Collectively they comprise the third most sexy, to counterfeit pharmaceutical drugs (Viagra, and Cialis)No. 1, and prostitution No.2. These estimated sales volumes are based on internet database Havoscope.

Chapter XIV
The Collapse

As I watched the USA vs. England women's soccer game for the World Cup championship, that old familiar sweet sound of our national anthem conjured up memories of long ago when I first carefully listened to the beauty of that song. Today, whenever I hear it as a prelude to an international sporting event—an Olympic or World Cup event where other countries are competing against the USA—that song sounds even sweeter than ever. To me, the words seem more pungent and purer when it's us (our nation, the United States of America) against the world. I feel the passion for victory when I see my country is challenged. With all its faults and shortcomings, it is still my home; and I love it.

American Made Apparel in essence has been eliminated, and we have lost a vital component of our industrial complex. Other industries are threatened at this very moment. We are importing seafood from China that would never pass our USDA standards, toys, and various electronics that have been proven defective.

Perhaps we should reconsider the long-term consequences of taking the cheapest route, because there is a definite downside to writing off whole industries like we have done for American Made Apparel. As we rethink our course of action, our commitment to society has to be questioned now, because it's not as simple as what is best for us individually, but what is best for us collectively. In this big picture we are no longer spectators rooting for our team to win, we have an active role to play, and if we don't understand our role, if we are in denial about our role, or simply fail to perform our role effectively, our team – America - loses.

I had the good fortune to be a member of an elite fitness club in Addison, TX - a northern suburb of Dallas - where the parking lot was sprinkled with expensive cars and several members drove Bentleys. Occasionally, you could spot a few of the Dallas Cowboys NFL Hall of Famers.

In the fitness club's luxury lounge right after my workout was where I met the new Dallas International Apparel Mart, in the person of a man. His name is James Baldwin, an international sourcing agent.

As we talked, we both vented about our biggest current challenges. He had just returned from China and Singapore where he visited factories that were manufacturing billions of dollars in apparel and accessories. His sourcing company had set them up for several of his large American manufacturing and retail clients.

I told James about my book "American Made Apparel" and he was intrigued, so I requested an interview to get a better perspective. About one week later, on a typical very warm summer's day, I visited my new acquaintance for the interview at his office. The tastefully decorated, but simple one-story suite of offices, in a quaint suburban Dallas office park, gives no impression of the $20 BILLION annually worth of merchandise this company was responsible for importing through their New York City showrooms and other network offices throughout Europe and Asia.

I had conflicting emotions concerning James Baldwin (the international sourcing agent). Part of me saw him as an enemy, because he was the replacement of entities that I had grown to love and cherish. My aunt's sewing shops, cutting contractors like Hubert Johnson and George Scales, the Apparel Mart; they are all gone. And the replacement is James Baldwin.

I had no reason to believe that James had anything to do with the collapse of American made apparel, and I knew that his job of importing apparel was going to be done by someone else if he wasn't there. James was enthusiastic about his role in the industry today. For me, it was kind of like talking to someone who is your replacement at a job that you really loved, and not only did they get a big raise at the job you had, but they are much more efficient than you were.

I was very fortunate to be able to meet someone like James, let alone interview him, so I adjusted my attitude towards him and straightened out my priorities. We talked about the Black Market, counterfeits and replicas fashion apparel and accessories. We talked for more than an hour about why the industry moved to offshore production, the likelihood of production ever coming back to America and what the circumstances would be for the US to ever regain a significant share of apparel manufacturing.

The essence of our discussion revealed that: One of the only ways the apparel production would return to the US in a significant way is that conventional seams in garments be either automated or fused by automation. The reason for this is because traditional piece goods (or apparel) production seams are labor intensive and factors heavily into the production cost of each garment.

It's unlikely that American workers will even want to compete with the extremely low labor rates of Asian countries. Yet there are innovative processes that can be utilized in garment construction that will circumvent the labor cost issue. James Baldwin identified the new sportswear manufacturer Under Armor as one of the successful innovators who are using advanced textiles to aid their production. The textile companies can play a bigger role in the manufacturing processes, yet there has to be a lot more co-ordination between the manufacturers and textile companies. They both need strong innovative leadership to do what has to be done, in order to regain a significant share of apparel production for the U.S.

The U.S. trade deficit with China means that U.S. companies that can't compete with ultra-low-priced Chinese goods must either lower their costs or go out of business. To lower their costs, many companies have started outsourcing to India and China, adding to U.S. unemployment. Other industries have simply dried up. U.S. manufacturing, as measured by the number of jobs, declined 21% between 1998 and 2008. As these industries declined, so has U.S. competitiveness in the global marketplace. (Source: BLS, Employees by Industry)

The United States Trade deficit with China currently **stands at $222Billion.**

Why Is There a U.S. Trade Deficit with China?

China is able to produce low-cost goods that Americans want. Most economists agree that China's competitive pricing is a result of two factors:

- A lower standard of living, which allows them to pay lower wages to workers.
- An exchange rate that is partially set to be always priced lower than the dollar.

How Can China Set Its Exchange Rate Lower than the Dollar?

China sets the value of its currency, the yuan, to always equal a set amount of a basket of currencies which includes the dollar. When the dollar loses value, China buys dollars through <u>U.S. Treasuries</u> to support it. In this way, the yuan's value is always within its targeted range. As long as the yuan's value is lower than the dollar, China's goods are cheaper in comparison.

Climate change Vs. Nanotechnology: Influences on future apparel.

In 1966 when Stanley Marcus predicted that in the future his store products would be sold over something, he called phonovision, it wasn't a lucky guess. He wasn't pulling a Nostradamus on us either. He was a very intelligent, well educated, and well-read man, who apparently knew that the semi-conductor industry was growing at a rapid pace.

As early as 1959 there were predictions being made about how the microprocessor would double in its power and speed, every 24 months. In 1965 the prediction that microprocessors would also shrink in size, as well as double its speed, and performance every 24 months was made by Intel Inc. co-founder Gordon Moore.

Intel is the largest most successful semiconductor manufacturer in America, and also number one in the world. This declaration is known as "Moore's Law" in the semiconductor industry, and it is said to have been accurate for four decades. However, that pace appears to have slowed down somewhat over the last 8 years, to 36 months instead of 24 months. Microprocessors which operate in relative obscurity for the most part, help make our daily life a breeze, by regulating traffic lights, our vehicles, our cell phones, home appliances such as microwave ovens, washers, and dryers, and last but not least or computers.

Over the last twenty years I have had the privilege and honor of working for the two largest semiconductor manufacturers in America. In doing so I have watched with great fascination and interest the emerging technology of our time: Nanotechnology, AKA nanotech is essentially the manipulation of matter, from a molecular and atomic level.

The very core of a cell gets manipulated, changing its physical properties to varying degrees, making it very different than it was in its original state. This technology has already produced some very impressive results in the early 2000s, such as stain resistant textiles, and clothing such as socks, and pants that have the capacity to cool the body.

The Under-Armour Sportswear manufacturer has highlighted a workout suit on its national TV advertisements that changes color at the flip of a switch. I also believe that the new nanotech textiles will have the capabilities to change not only colors, but certain patterns like pin stripes, plaids, herringbone, and hound's-tooth, as well.

I interviewed James Baldwin in 2010, and we made our predictions over two years before we saw the Under-Armour TV commercials. Nanotechnology is a growing global market that the National Science Foundation estimates will be worth a trillion dollars by 2022.

Meanwhile, commercial applications continue to spread. Homeowners can now buy windows manufactured by PPG Industries, a company that uses nanoscale particles of titanium dioxide to make glass that doesn't streak and never needs washing. Food companies have started experimenting with Nano packaging that changes color when food spoils or contains bacteria like E. coli. The prefix has even spread into popular culture, where Apple named its new music player iPod Nano digital.

There is however a very significant obstacle to nanotech products in the marketplace, and that is the threat of direct health hazards of inhaling the microscopic particles, and biological contamination to the environment. Both of which have potentially lethal consequences. Today there are intensive research and development programs underway to resolve the issue of making nanotech more environmentally secure, and far less of a health hazard when ingested.

Nanotechnology is currently being used to produce a whole new generation of fuel-efficient aircraft (because it is fifty to a hundred times stronger than steel, yet one-sixth the weight), and countless medical and electronics innovations have been discovered. It's only a matter of time before it produces big changes in the big world of fashion apparel.

The pressures of climate change will be a driving force in the acceptance of fashion apparel made with nanotech fabrics.

I make a conscious effort to be open minded about most everything. There are lyrics in one of my favorite songs by Quincy Jones that goes "there are not many things in life you can be sure of, except rain falls from the clouds, sun lights up the sky, and hummingbirds do fly".

An attorney friend of mine, who shall remain nameless, is an heir to a wealthy family business in Dallas, and he asked me an interesting question one day. He (happened to be a White man) asked me "what was the most repugnant experience you ever had in your professional life?" I replied "wow, there are a lot of them, I have to think about it for a minute. How about you? What was the most repugnant experience in your professional life"? He told me that his most repugnant experience was witnessing a

Federal Judge collude with an Attorney, against a Litigant in his courtroom. This should have shocked me I guess, but it did not, because it just reminded me that I was a Litigant who had been unjustly slammed by a Federal Judge in a case where the evidence was conspicuously and overwhelmingly in my favor. This is a typical experience in most American courtrooms, whether you are a litigant, a defendant, or a dead victim like Trayvon Martin, when you wear the skin, I'm in. Far too often equal justice under the law does not exist for African American males.

One of my biggest joys in life is to have had the experience of leading a corporate board of eight luminaries for a Washington DC non-profit educational consulting organization. I personally recruited all eight people; four of which were Ph.Ds.

Not only because of their stellar credentials and brilliant minds, they were an absolute delight to work with. This was during a time when people looked for reasons to work together, instead of looking for reasons not to.

Our volunteer group focused on character development, through the emphasis of Crime and Violence Prevention educational programs (workshops, and seminars) for inner-city high school students, and faculty. We also produced educational videos featuring star NFL, and NBA players including NBA 1992 Rookie of the Year Larry Johnson.

Most of the participating students were athletes, including several high-profile basketball, and football stars who went on to the NBA, and NFL like three NBA players Jalen Rose, Vashon Lenard, and Howard Isley in one Detroit class, and Chauncy Billups in Denver.

We also produced educational videos to convey our curriculum's basic philosophy. In this process there was a strong emphasis on "Commitment to society". We stressed love, and respect for our nation, because it is the greatest country on earth, and it avails its citizens many terrific opportunities for a high quality of life, liberty, and the pursuit of happiness.

The greed factor in our society threatens to subvert our way of life as much as, if not more than radical Islamic terrorist. It is a rampant and insidious thread in the social fabric of our culture, manifesting itself in many politicians from the municipal levels, to the state, and even federal levels being convicted of under the table financial crimes. City Council members, Mayors, Congressmen, Senators, and Governors all across the nation unfortunately prove my point that greed threatens to undermine a higher quality of life for our society as a whole.

The Wall Street, and high finance criminals like Bernie Madoff emphasize my point even more. The fact is that there are many more that don't play by the rules yet haven't been caught.

The wealth gap between the super-rich and the middle class which continues to expand at a rapid pace, threatens to suppress incentive for millions of hard-working Americans. The Occupy Wall Street movement had it right when they declared that it is not right for millionaires to pay a smaller percentage in taxes than the working poor, and middle-class citizens.

The fact that Billionaire Warren Buffet – one of the richest men in the world - agreed with the Occupy movement in a highly publicized statement underscored the urgency of this lingering problem. What Mr. Buffet said is that he believes it is wrong that he pays a smaller percentage of income tax than his secretary, although he makes a whole lot more than her (this is a understatement his net worth is over $53Billion).

The fact is that many of the super–rich pay little or no taxes at all because of loopholes, and offshore investment accounts which are not taxable by law. The super-rich became a lot richer during the worst economic recessions in U.S. history, because many corporations increased their profits by cutting their staffs and forcing workers who still had jobs to take on more work.

They manipulated the vast sums of money in offshore investments, rather than attempting to help get the country back on its feet. Under these circumstances it's difficult for people who know the truth, to stand before teenage students and tell them with a straight face that they should have a commitment to our society, play by the rules, avoid the common pitfalls of crime and violence, work and study hard and they will be rewarded with a higher quality of life.

We ask our troops from all over this country, all races, and all genders, to sacrifice their lives for this country if necessary, in military conflicts. Our troops accept the challenge of defending our country with the promise that we all have equal opportunities here and far too often our government has failed to keep that promise of equal opportunity.

We have to find a way to tap, and nurture responsible leadership that will push the technology envelope. We have the resources to organize our collective capital and human assets, so that we more effectively utilize the new technologies at our disposal, to benefit the fabric of our society as a whole.

There are eleven million, millionaires in the U.S.A. and well over 300 million who fall below the millionaire status, according to reliable sources. Just like my former employer Stanley Marcus recognized that the quality of life in the culture of Dallas would be enhanced by the inclusion of previously disenfranchised minorities, so to must the super-rich recognize this reality.

It is virtually inevitable that the Occupy movement or a surrogate re-emerge to champion economic equality because of the continual widening economic gap between the super-rich and the middle-class.

The stark contrast in the widening wealth gap crushes incentive for the masses of people in the middle class. In the Genesis of this book I focused on the pre-civil rights 1950's plight of African-American families throughout rural Texas, and how the families with the most able bodies to work the cotton fields, made more money by pulling their resources together and cooperating with each other.

The little boys and girls who were too young to pull their own bags, still contributed by bringing water to the other family members in the field. Even though their contribution may not have been as valuable as an adolesant, or adult who could manage to pick a lot more cotton, they were all in it together, and relied on each other's contribution for the benefit of their family.

That legacy is something we should never forget, when we do our whole culture's social fabric is weakened by it.

Just so my point about equal opportunities gets a clearer optic, the Xerox Corporation offers a truly brilliant example of diversity and equal employment opportunities. I consider myself very fortunate to have been one of the many African American professionals in the big influx of the 1970s at Xerox Office Products division in Dallas. Xerox was the absolute pinnacle of diversity and equal employment opportunity in corporate America.

The rewards were great for the employer and employee as well, and Xerox continues a successful legacy prevailing against a massive onslaught of competition from Japanese copier makers in the 1980's. Many of my former colleagues excelled before, during and after they worked at Xerox. They did so because they had real opportunities that included mentors, and customized support systems to enhance their chances for success, the same as many of their White counterparts.

The list of African American luminaries who worked at Xerox includes Barry Rand, CEO of AARP, James Brown, CBS Sports (NFL Today anchor) - both of Washington DC -, & Gene Ruffin a Xerox executive from El Segundo, CA who was promoted to Vice President in Dallas.

We had bold and aggressive leadership from a brilliant young President - Don Massaro - who was thirty something at the time and went on to make big innovations in the computer technology evolution. There were Plant Managers like Ty Kelly, and Phil Nolan, Engineers like John Carroll, Executives like Brooks Fitch, and Jim Lee, and Directors like Marvin Robinson, who was my Manager's, Manager, and many others who held key administrative positions like Leah Woodson.

I have worked in corporate America for over four decades spanning 18 major cities coast to coast, from Intel Inc. to Texas Instruments, IBM, McDonnel-Douglas, (now Boeing), Mobil Oil, Sun Oil, Dow Chemical, former telecom giant MCI, The United States Congress on Capitol Hill, and four of the top five engineering firms in the nation, just to name a few.

If I had not experienced working at Xerox, I would not know what real diversity and equal employment opportunity looked like. Today in 2015 far too many people are totally comfortable with their workforce having 1% or less African Americans employed, like my profession, and in many offices 0%. We are not 1% of the soldiers that put their lives on the line for this country every day. African Americans comprise 14% of the nation's population. The current employment picture for African American males is worse than the late 70's and is not acceptable.

Moreover, this analysis brought to mind the lesson that we red-blooded Americans could learn from our sports team. Team is first, for real sports fans, and it should be for all citizens in the context of our nation as a whole. The dynamic works kind of like this; Our Professional sports teams, of which I am a big fan, are made up from people of all races, nationalities, and religions.

The former NBA Champion Los Angeles Lakers (still my favorite) had an all-star forward (Pau Gasol), from Spain, and Laker fans of all races cheer for him just as hard as any of his other teammates, from New Jersey, or Philadelphia. He contributed to the success of the team in a big way. The fans knew it, and that's what matters most to them.

The former NBA Champion San Antonio Spurs had star players from France Tony Parker, Boris Diaw; and Argentina, Manu Ginobli that Spurs fans love, and cheer for, simply because they helped the Spurs win. We have got to get over the dumb stuff, and support people that help our nation win, regardless of the skin they are in.

Chapter XV

Epilogue

This book is a salute to my Aunt Margaret, and Aunt Connie. It started out in concept, as a magazine article focusing on my three Aunts (now 97 years old, the other 91, and one deceased) and the terrific craftsmanship they produced, sewing dresses for Howard Wolff, Victor Costa, and their contracts with Neiman-Marcus.

I met a small-time magazine staffer at an Ed Hardy "Christian Audigier", fashion show held at the Palladium in Dallas. We talked about each other's background in the fashion world. When he found out about my experience as a men's sportswear designer, and my aunts experience of sewing for many of the top retail stores in the industry, he expressed an exuberant interest in doing a magazine article.

I told my aunts about his interest. They were pleased that their hard work and superb craftsmanship would be recognized, even in a rather obscure magazine that only catered to local hair salons.

After a few follow up calls to the magazine staffer - who actually worked in the art selection area, and was not really a writer – with no response from him, I told my aunts that I would write the article myself, and send it out to several much more prominent magazines.

After a few months period of time in contemplating just how to proceed with the scope, and focus of the article, bits and pieces of sentimental memories began to emerge. Those memories continued to emerge over months, and ultimately four years, and now we've got it, "American Made Apparel, The Legacy-The Collapse".

This salute also goes out to all those Americans who just like us enjoyed seeing happy customers wearing clothes that we made.

From the Cutters who plotted out the most efficient use of the fabric, laid the patterns, marked them, and cut them with precision, to the people who made and sold the buttons and zippers, and even the thread, to the pattern makers and designers like me; we salute you, and we celebrate you. You are the last of an American breed.

Your time in the business of making apparel may be gone, but you are not forgotten. You and only you know what it feels like to see happy clients wearing the high quality, and beautiful fruits of your labor, and your passion. I feel you, and I celebrate you.

While making a delivery for Neiman-Marcus in Bryan Towers - a downtown Dallas office building - I discovered this beautiful, timeless work of poetry that I fell in love with at first sight. I was seventeen years old then, over forty years later it is still my favorite today. I want to share it with you below:

Desiderata

Go placidly amid the noise and haste,
and remember what peace there may be in silence.
As far as possible without surrender
be on good terms with all persons.
Speak your truth quietly and clearly;
and listen to others,
even the dull and the ignorant;
they too have their story.

Avoid loud and aggressive persons,
they are vexations to the spirit.
If you compare yourself with others,
you may become vain and bitter;
for always there will be greater and lesser persons than yourself.
Enjoy your achievements as well as your plans.

Keep interested in your own career, however humble;
it is a real possession in the changing fortunes of time.
Exercise caution in your business affairs;
for the world is full of trickery.
But let this not blind you to what virtue there is;
many persons strive for high ideals;
and everywhere life is full of heroism.

Be yourself.
Especially, do not feign affection.
Neither be cynical about love;
for in the face of all aridity and disenchantment
it is as perennial as the grass.

Take kindly the counsel of the years,
gracefully surrendering the things of youth.
Nurture strength of spirit to shield you in sudden misfortune.
But do not distress yourself with dark imaginings.
Many fears are born of fatigue and loneliness.
Beyond a wholesome discipline,
be gentle with yourself.

You are a child of the universe,
no less than the trees and the stars;
you have a right to be here.
And whether or not it is clear to you,
no doubt the universe is unfolding as it should.

Therefore be at peace with God,
whatever you conceive Him to be,
and whatever your labors and aspirations,
in the noisy confusion of life keep peace with your soul.
With all its sham, drudgery, and broken dreams,
it is still a beautiful world.
Be cheerful.
Strive to be happy.

My mother – Johnnie Mae Wooten and my cousin Duane Thomas; former Dallas Cowboys Running Back and Super Bowl VI Champion. Photo taken five months after Super Bowl VI. (Controversial Super Bowl VI MVP)

In memoriam of my Great-Great Grandfather, Samuel Beecham, who was abducted from the streets of Baltimore, MD as a free man in the mid 1800's taken to Texas and sold into slavery by several evil white men who connived him into helping them with a simple chore, and then subdued him.

Samuel Beecham is gone but not forgotten. How I wish he could see this book, and see his Great-Grand Daughters who were world-class Seamstresses, and Great-Great Grandchildren who have in their ranks a very successful and prominent Attorney, a Brigadier General, a Super Bowl Champion, a good Designer, and very good Basketball Player.

I wish he could see all the successful School Teachers, Preachers, Entrepreneurs, Hair Stylist, Soldiers, and Sailors in our family. Of course, none of the aforementioned successes would be possible without the sacrifice of many honest hard-working loving and nurturing family members like my mother, who are the glue that held our family together since Samuel Beecham arrived in Texas over 150 years ago.